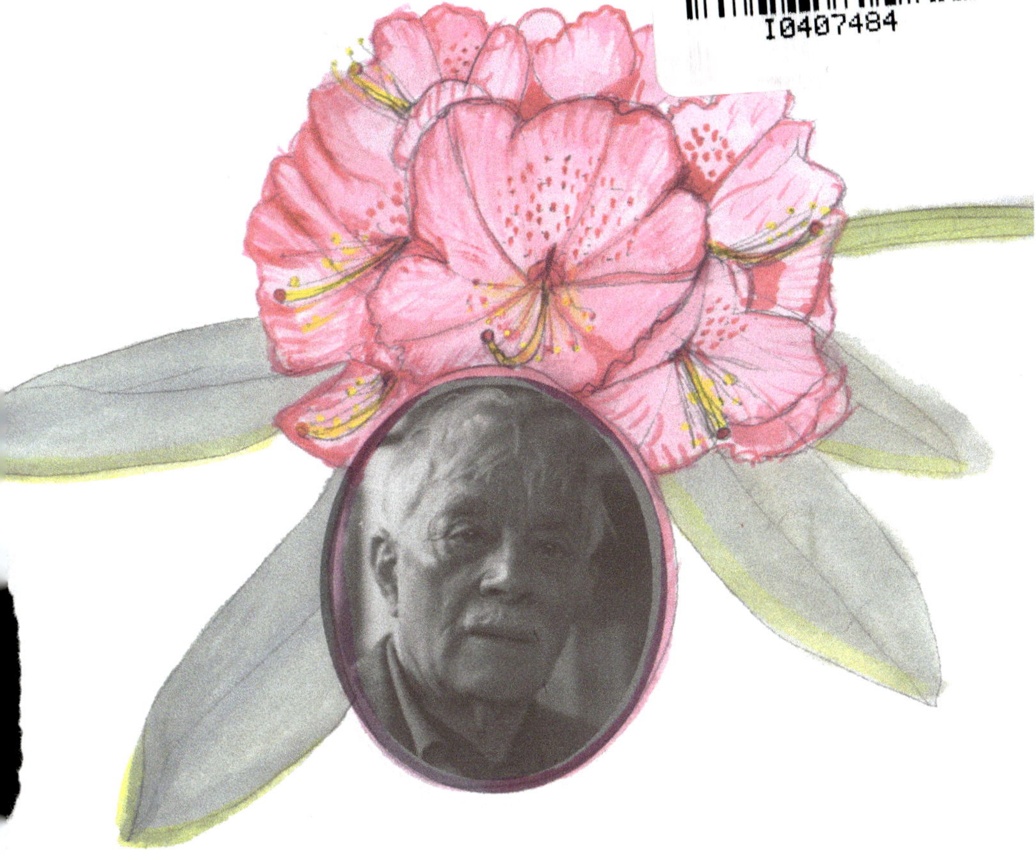

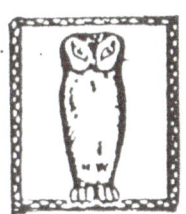

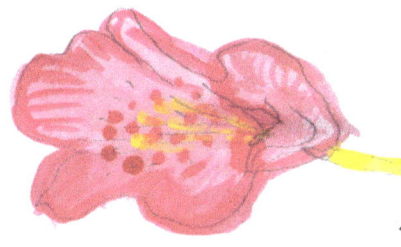

dedicated to Henry

Cover Design + Artwork + Layout and Design
Bee Williamson of Bee's Boutique Books
www.beesboutiquebooks.biz

Printed and Bound in Australia by BookPOD

This book is available for purchase from:
www.bookpod.com.au

National Library of Australia
Cataloguing-in-Publication entry

Author: Williamson, Bee.

Title: Nature : a gift / Bee Williamson.

Edition: 1st ed.

ISBN: 978-0-646-56174-5 (pbk.)

Dewey Number: A821.4

Contact Bee at: bee@hive.id.au
to purchase artworks:
www.hive.id.au

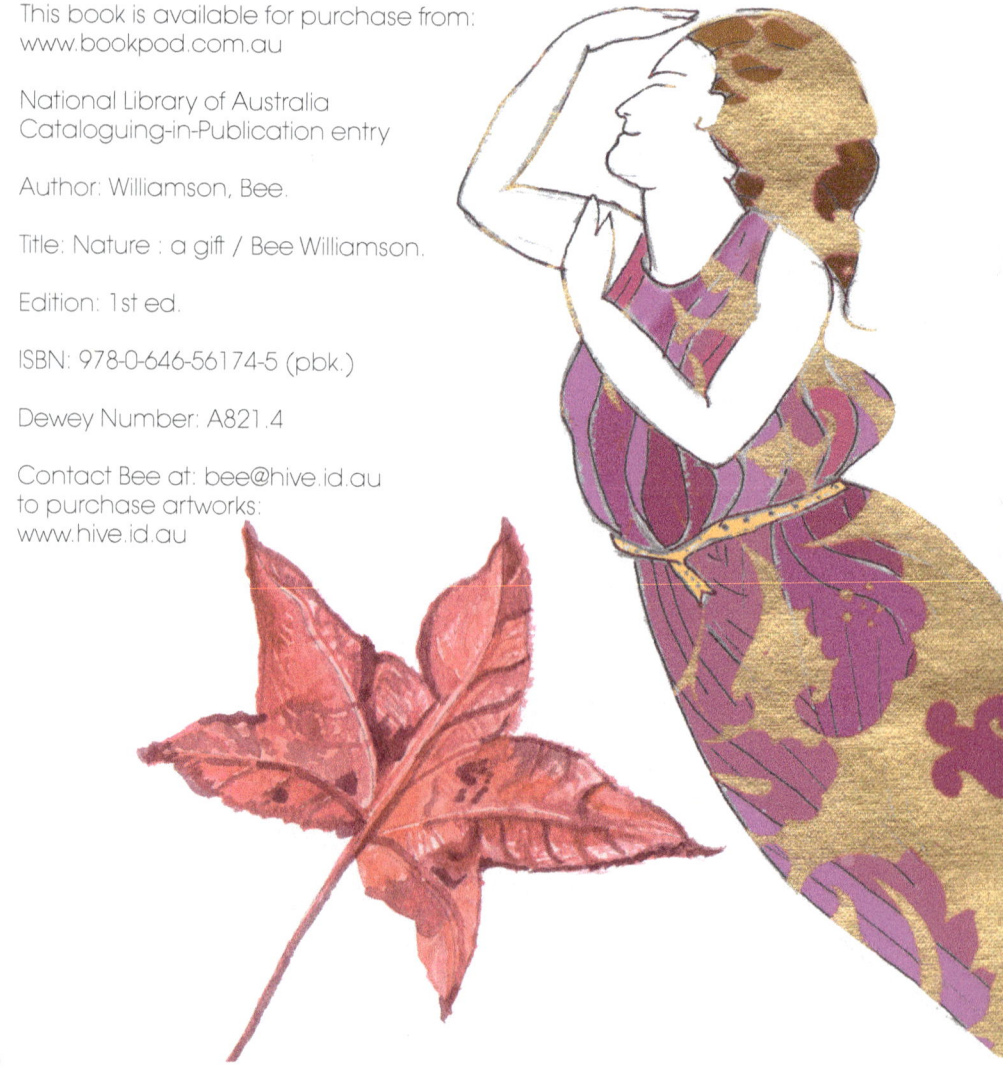

Introduction

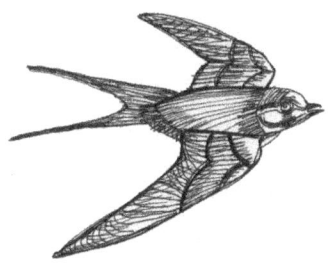

This book is about our birthright, the gift. The gift is both a spiritual truth and a mystery. Nature is that gift. In the same way our bodies are a gift from Great Spirit. But we have degraded nature, until it has become just a resource to be emptied, used and exploited. And we are losing the connection between ourselves and nature. It is the right path to take to honour, love and protect nature. Farmers who have not lost the connection are well aware of this. To exploit our earth as just 'a thing', an "object" to get the most out of, to be extracted and carved up, is something that most native cultures see as a bizarre and strange attitude. American Indian and indigenous Australians know we don't own the land, we belong to her. We behave as if we are alienated from our planet, the Earth that supports life itself. We reap what we sow. The seeds we are planting are alienation and estrangement from that which gives life. We are born 'in' to the family of humanity. We are born 'in' to the wondrous realm of Nature.

As we go about our daily work, we are often caught up in the mindless acquiring of wealth. To seek only to acquire money, for no real purpose than to have more money, leaves our earth at the mercy of economies and industries that, in the long run, may not serve our interests or the interests of the planet. While our backs are turned, what happens to mother nature? As a culture we can sometimes be blind to the consequences of our actions and choices. Long-term health for humanity is bound intimately to the health of our natural world.

With these troubling issues in mind, it became clear - I had to write this book. But how? Where to start? "Why don't you write a book of nature poems and illustrate them?" said my grandfather Henry in spirit. The journey began by enrolling in botanical Illustration classes at the Royal Botanical Gardens, Melbourne. The majority of poems were written during my six months as poet-in-residence at Pheast48 café in Armadale. I invite you to join me on my journey through *Nature - a gift*.

Bee Williamson

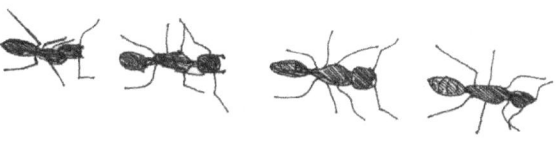

3

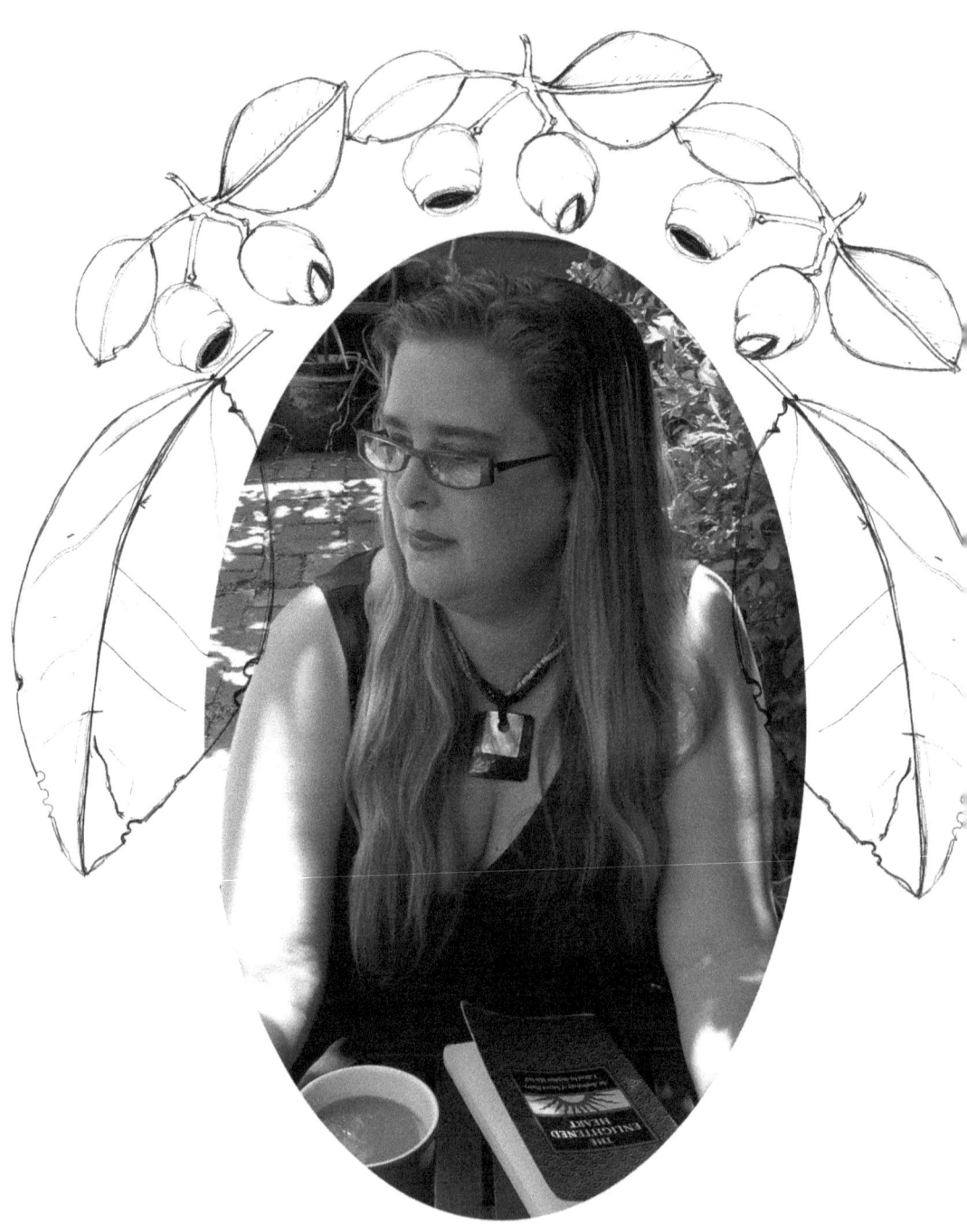

Biography

All true artists, whether they know it or not, create from a place of no-mind, from inner stillness. Eckhart Tolle

My artwork is about the process. For me it is 'meditation in action'. I enjoy quietening the mind and just feeling the brush on the canvas, pen on paper. This year's poems started as an expression of my love of nature. Sometimes nature is my only solace.

Living with a mental illness for the last twelve years has simplified my approach to art, bringing my expression truer to my heart. Birds, trees and the nature spirits guide me in my day-to-day life. They are my true friends when everything seems bleak.

Coming from a family of artists, I am fortunate to have side-stepped excessive intellectulisation of my art practice and, since graduating from the Victorian College of the Arts, have not been asked to limit my creativity. My spiritual connection to my paternal grandfather Henry Williamson, who was a prolific writer and naturalist and sometimes called 'The Last Romantic', is a source of great comfort and eccentric inspiritation.

Nature is my friend and my protector. The main themes in my artwork up till now have been women, dance and flowers. Like most artists and writers, I hold a fascination for detail. Alone in the school yard, sitting for hours, just studying a daisy.

The collection of artwork, now known as "Nature - a gift", is made up of pen and ink, watercolour, acrylic on canvas and photography. Influences on this work are Melbourne's own Mirka Mora and Pablo Picasso's 'Vollard Suite'. I also adore the work of the Pre-Raphaelites, Symbolists and Art Nouveau. Since 2003 my artwork has enjoyed twenty exhibitions around Melbourne. Many of the artworks are in this, my second book. My first "The Hidden Self" (2009) was a co-publication with Naomi Downie.

the mad man, the lover, and the poet, all have ways of knowing. Shakespeare

5

CONTENTS

List of Poems

List of Artworks & Photography

Where We Belong.

Where do you really belong
when nature is not your friend?

Where is your heaven imagined
If nature is not paradise?

Why are there gardeners in every home
when the rich soil is not a pleasure to hold?

In our street the trees are friends
laden with gifts
Plums
Apples
Lemons
Pears
Cumquats

Every fruit we find is from
The friend who doesn't hide
Its strength
Or
Its vulnerability

A friend who speaks only
To those who listen
And is silent in the
Moon's presence

A friend who finds you weary
And feeds you figs
taking you in
curling its leaves
into a small bower of pale green
lifting your eyes
skyward

A friend whose
steadfastness is not under question
From anyone

A friend whose giving
Is like breathing
As natural as a smile on a baby
eating sweets

When we are in a forest
we are among good company
company that never doubts
your soul, heart and mind.
But will doubt your intentions
depending on chainsaws

When you are friends with trees
You are friends with the world!
Anywhere you go
There is your friend!

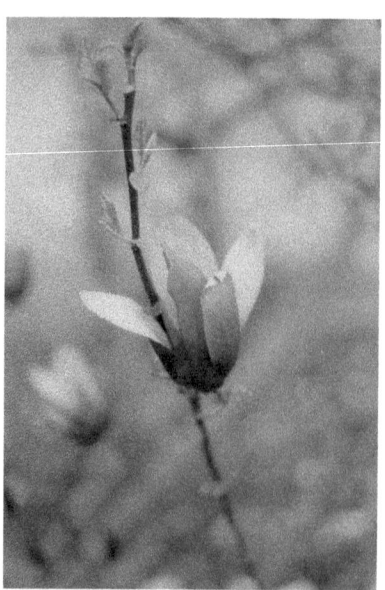

Where We Belong.

9

When we are lush.

Like our brother
The red rhododendron
It is in a tree's nature
To give

These things of solidified light
Light which comes from the heavens
Are friends
Who find us weeping
And know
That a small cherry blossom
Is all our heart desires

In nature we find
Our soul
In the quiet language-less space
Of worms, ants, bees and trees
We find our
Knowing fathers in the ancient Wisdom Trees
The ones that were here before our city
Geared us into twenty first century gluttony

"I am your friend, do not fear me"
says the iron bark gum, wanting only
to know which way to grow
between the power lines

When the cocoa you eat is from a tree
That grew despite your not knowing its name
That is Nature's gift
Just because you might not see it
or know it

Like the food that sustains
Us
The beauty of a perfect pink camellia
Sipped daily
Renews our spirits

When we are lush
the scarlet rose
grown in quiet contemplation
Will be a friend for life.

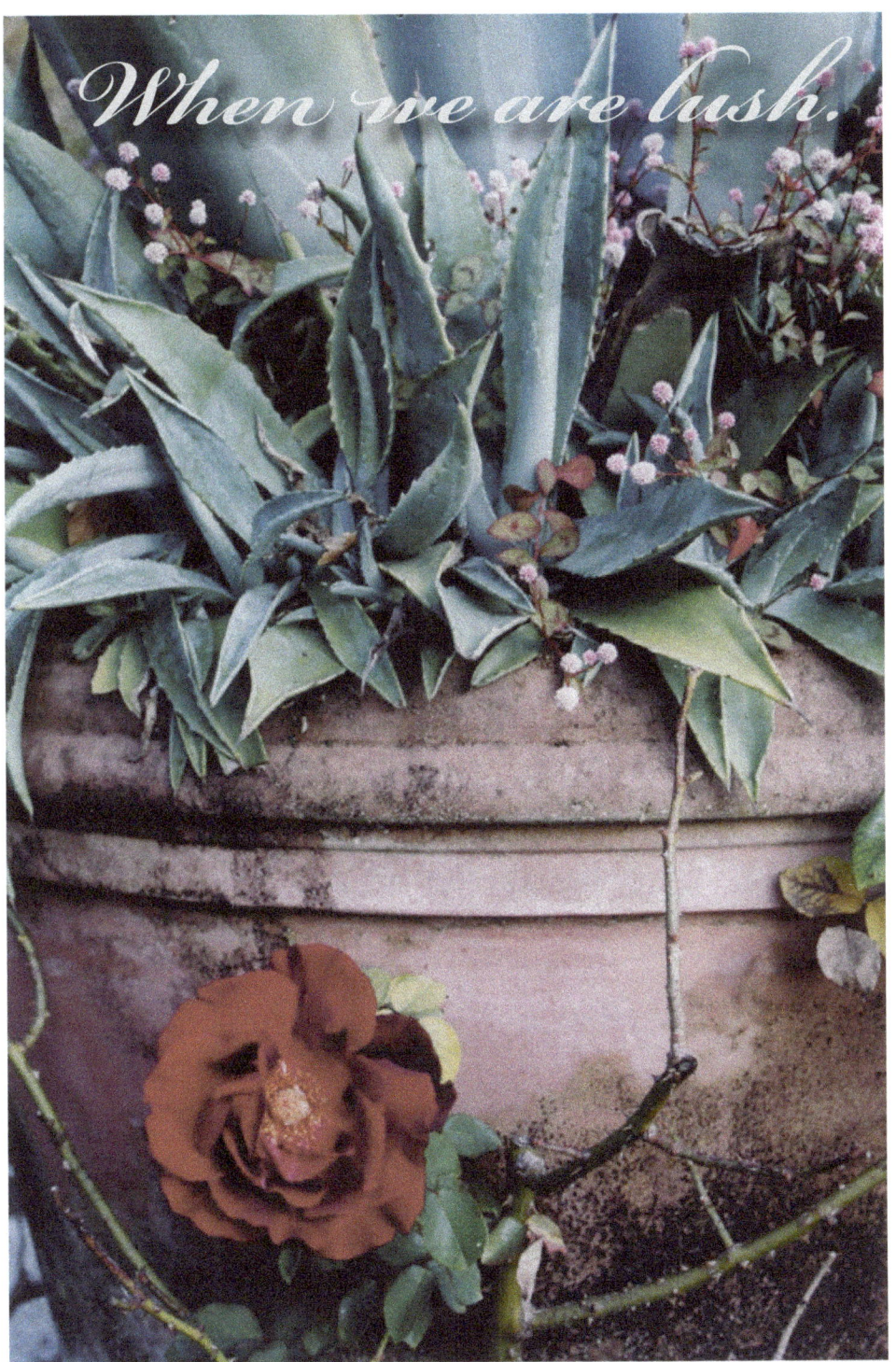

When we are lush.

Then.

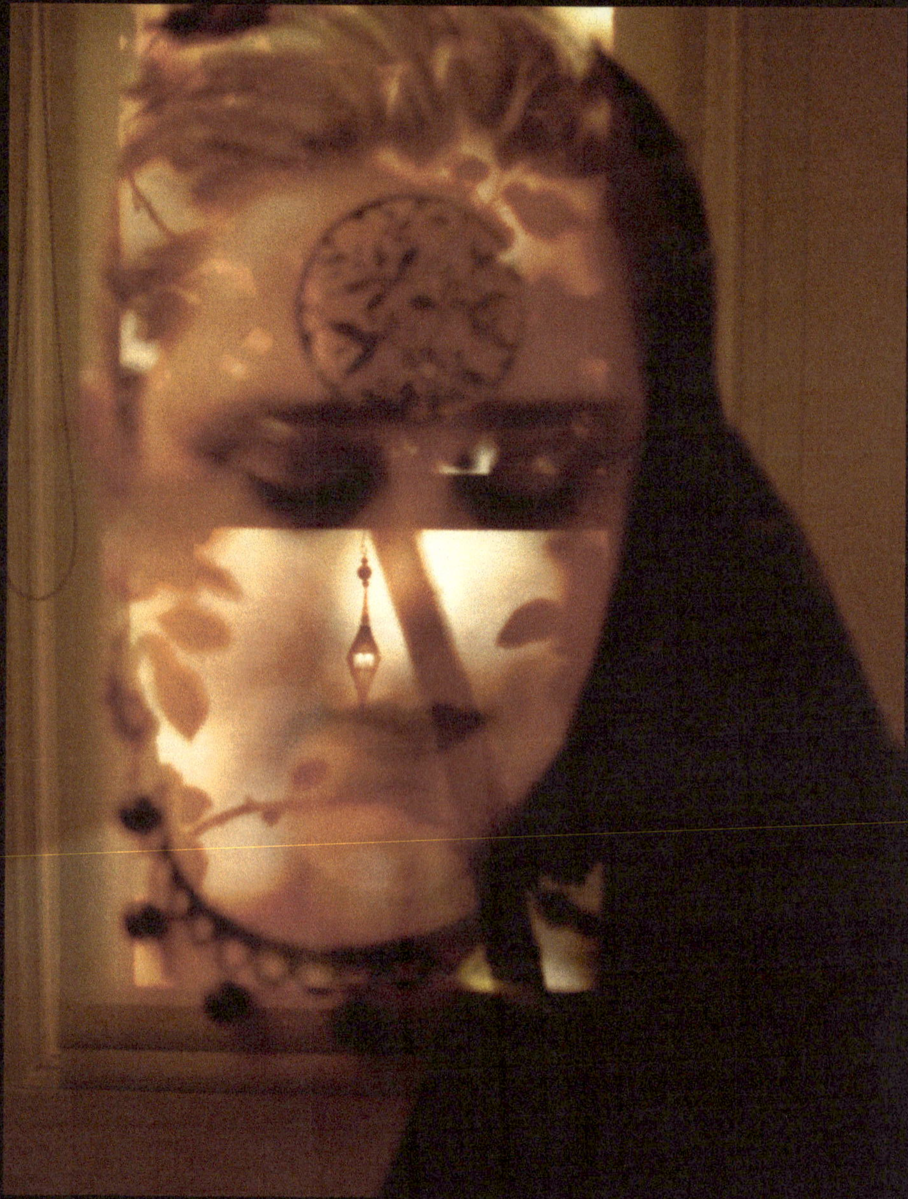

Then.

I lay with you
Among the peach & avocado trees
I breathed the smoke
Deep into my lungs
Nude & reading
Anaïs Nin
in the sun

you are no longer my friend
the one who called me 'lazy'
after days alone
in a locked padded cell
barely breathing
'lazy' I was when I didn't know you wanted me
but you didn't seem to mind
then.

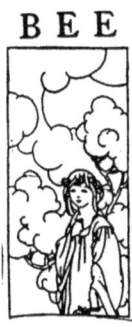

B E E

A Field of Dahlias.

when you think of paradise
what do you see?
I see a field of dahlias, heads high and open to the wind
of a lush garden of fruits
of a warm familiar hand cradling a tea mug
the feeling of being held in an embrace
that stills the chattering mind
a mind that knows no end of selfishness

these things are not priced, like a life, at a dollar an hour
these pleasures are not controlled by markets
and shareholders
I am not winning because you are losing
I am not gaining from your slavery

when I hear of a young man's suicide in China
a young man weary and beside himself
in slavery to the machine of capitalism
I weep
lying in bed
completely overwhelmed with guilt
that my choices
are   my ipod his nickel stains
his   my leather purse his tannery stench
chores   our cheap rice his gangrenous infection

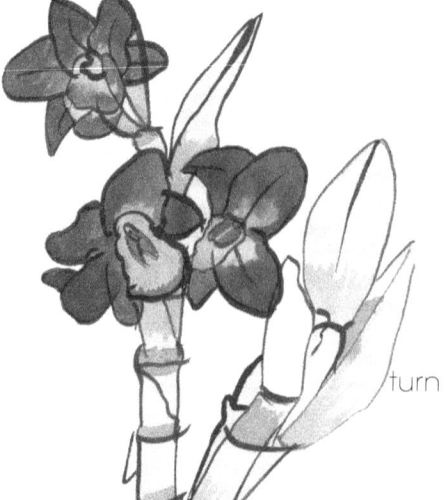

a field of dahlias at Ripponlea
my first world paradise
a world
that has no inbuilt conclusion
but that we say goodbye to
when our heart or lungs or mind
cease their tired obligations
to continue life

where we breathe the same air
as twelfth-century mystic poets
turn the same soil as our grandmother
turned with her same love
for the peace rose
the violet petunia
and the humble geranium.

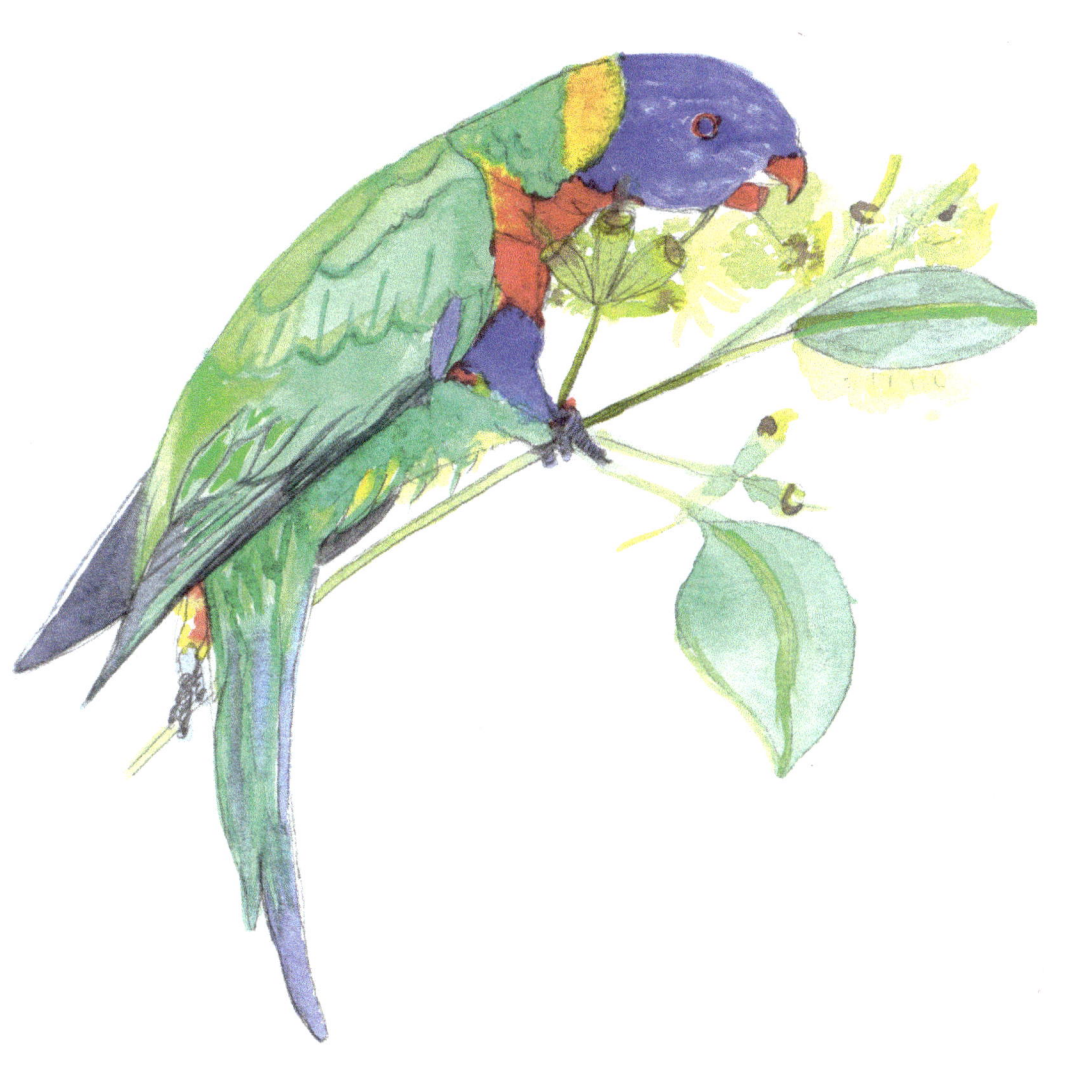

A Field of Dahlias.

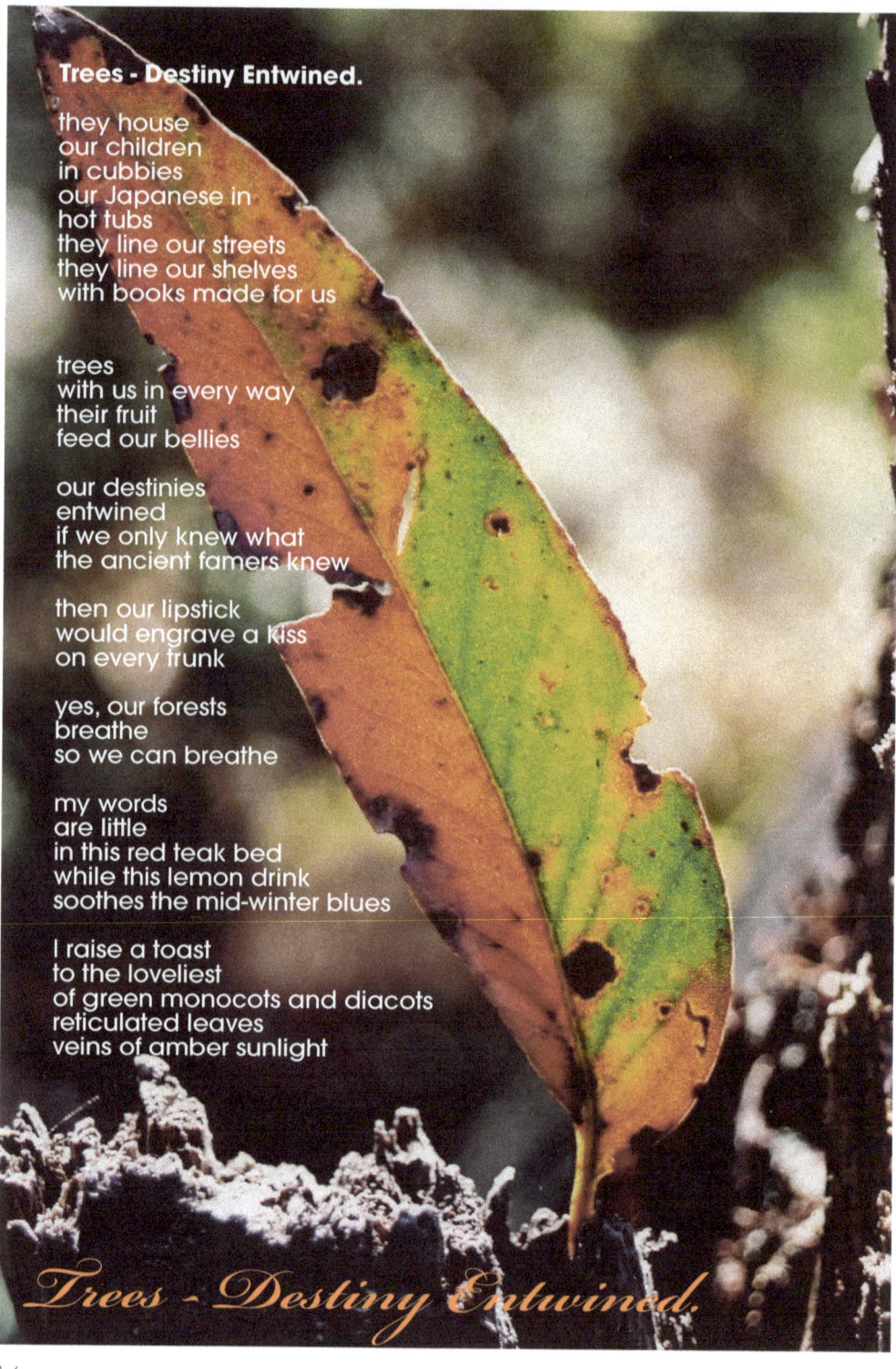

Trees - Destiny Entwined.

they house
our children
in cubbies
our Japanese in
hot tubs
they line our streets
they line our shelves
with books made for us

trees
with us in every way
their fruit
feed our bellies

our destinies
entwined
if we only knew what
the ancient famers knew

then our lipstick
would engrave a kiss
on every trunk

yes, our forests
breathe
so we can breathe

my words
are little
in this red teak bed
while this lemon drink
soothes the mid-winter blues

I raise a toast
to the loveliest
of green monocots and diacots
reticulated leaves
veins of amber sunlight

Trees - Destiny Entwined.

swollen with sap
september
like a mother's belly
filled with blossom

like God's painting
autumn
all the dusky reds and oranges
of a japanese maple
full of the love of her existence
brimming with quiet jubilee
each leaf waving in the breeze
like a happy child's hand

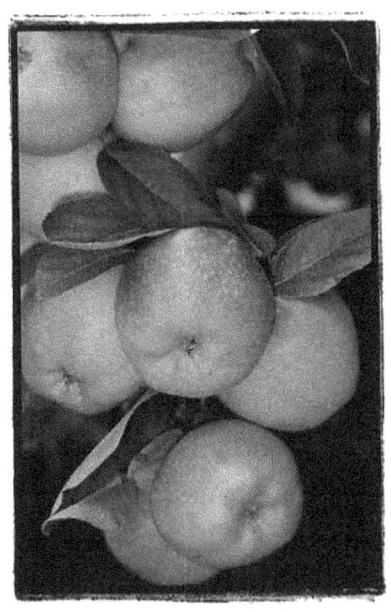

soft and marble-like
our ghost gums
stretching ever moonward
in their splendour

our shadows
of useless fears
seem small
when the grass dies
and the fleeing wildlife cry
their echos vanish in the fire
nature's plan seems invisible
till the first native seeds *crack*!
and green shoots sprout on black bark

our origins
are bound
inextricably together

with each turn of the hemispheres
I am learning
that my place
in nature
is "in".
we were born 'in'

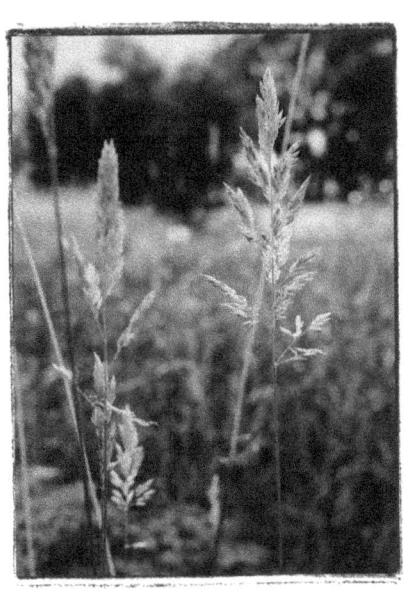

our destinies
entwined.

17

To Fly.

swooping
soaring
above the Earth
how you must trust
those wings of yours

to see
the forest
expand below you

in the darkness of dawn
I have soared with the birds
in my night dreams
across Germany
a flock of birds
showing me
how to navigate
over the countryside
using the magnetic leylines

how I could learn

as they trust
only
their own

power

effort

energy.

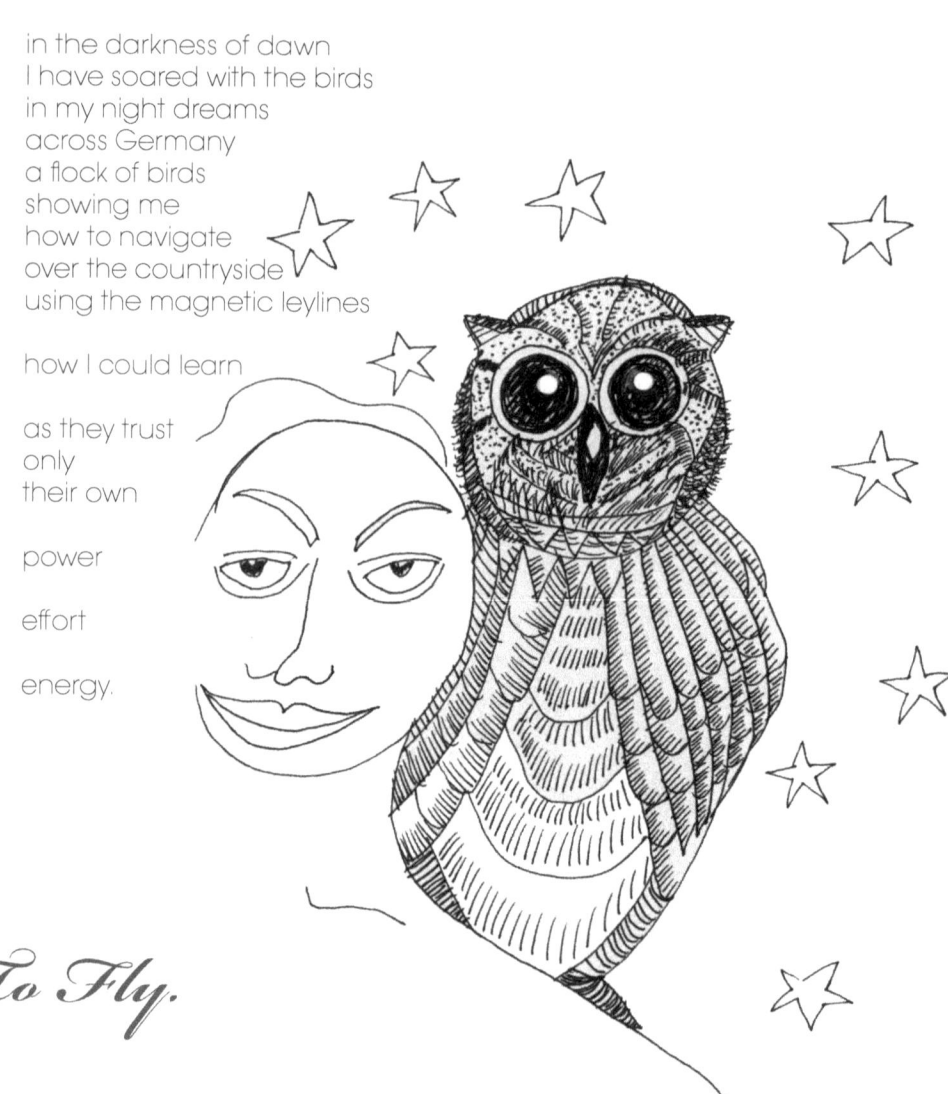

To Fly.

Beauty's Hand.

lying like Thumbelina
on the thin rim
of a plum-hued petal
I am trembling

the unsettling of everything
afraid to be left behind
with only my shadow's faith

any sanctuary I find
lies effortlessly
on the deep blush of a burgundy rose
on the iridescent
blue-melting-to-purple eye
of a peacock's feather

Beauty's hand is God's hand

held in
the cold solidity
of rose quartz
which turns over
warm
in my hand.

for Brenda Alexis

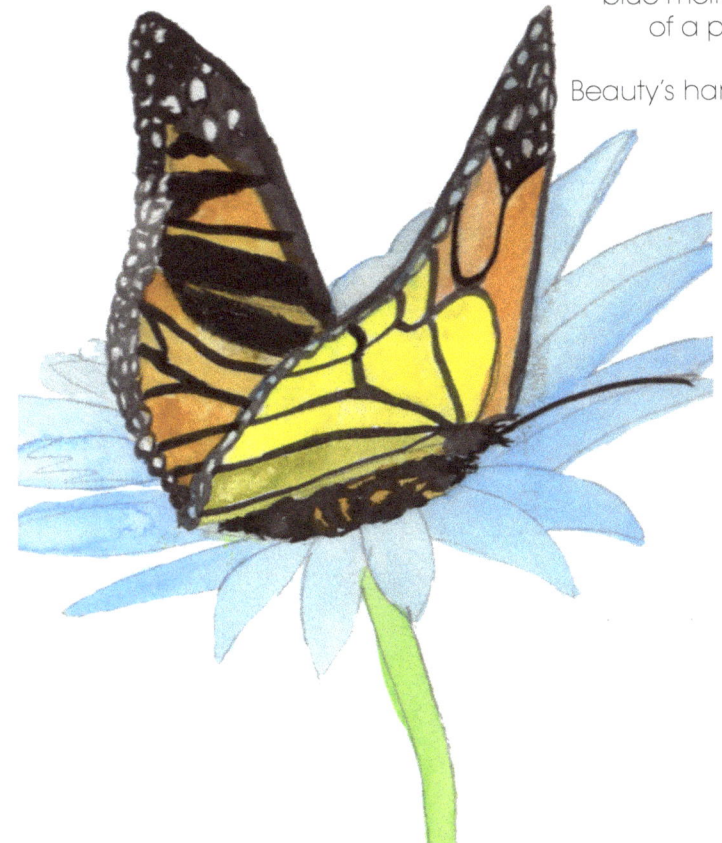

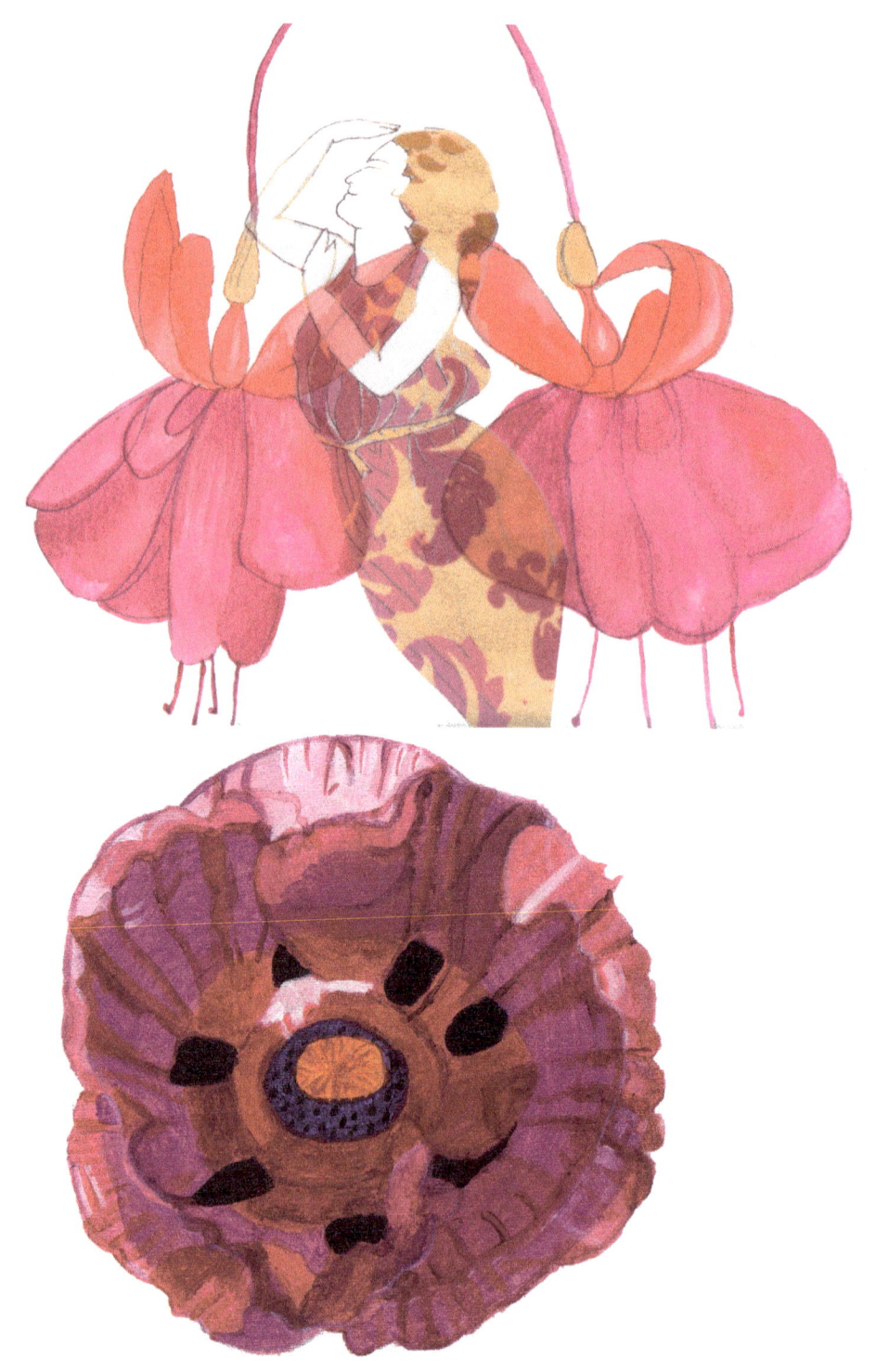

Maribel.

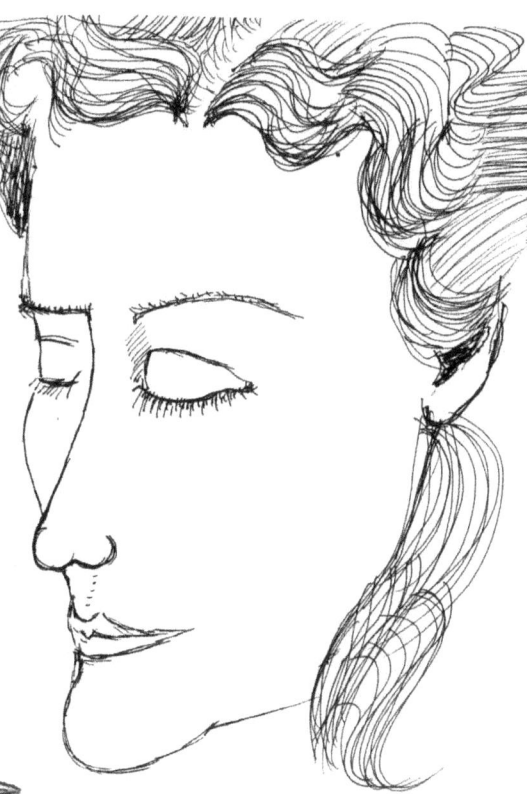

maribel.

in her blossoming garden
each stem lovingly crafted
to fit a vision of beauty
as fine as any artist

a curve of soft lilac
a scent of French lavender
saffron petals of marigold
daisies in the folds
of her frou-frou dresses

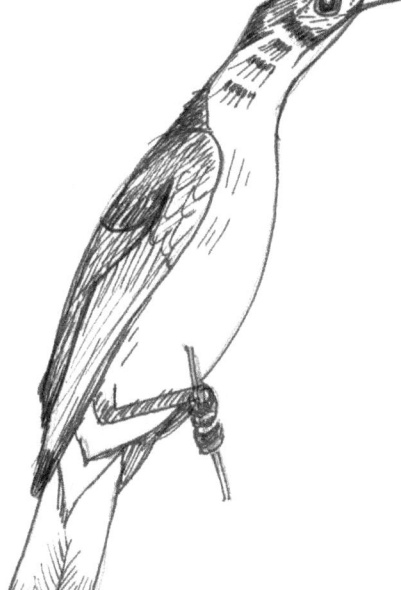

bending to feel
the world
touching a hue
known only to
you

the highlands cabin
with apple and wisteria
and half-wild horses
are home to this
Nature's daughter

she lies at night
a soft caress
her lover's face
abandoned to
a darkness like outer space.

Everything You Have Loved.

Everything you have loved
I have loved too

The women you've cherished
have cherished me

The music that enveloped your soul
touched mine

The ragged cliffs, coastlines and desolate moors
of your childhood
were the rough Celtic sea tides
of my birth place

I have traveled with you across continents
across time zones, language changes and cultural shifts

Your blue eyes
glassy grey when sick
are my blue eyes

I remember physics by the sea at half moon bay
lost to worlds of rockpools together
where 'all the elements come together'
earth, air, fire and water

I remember Glastonbury
staring up at the stage, muddy cold feet, looking at you
then turning around to see thousands of faces
staring at the stage, wondering why -
there's only Harry & Gilli up there?

Crazy times of flying fox falls, crashes on sleds into Georgeham,
speeding like maniacs on the icy roads
bitter apples for the walk to school
six a.m. veggie patch raids on snow pea vines
Easter egg hunts when I swore I saw a real bunny!

exotic fruits galore in Bali, hot chilli soup I hated
a naughty monkey on Orlando's head
we all braved Garuda together
with a welcome home vomit from us kids on the steps of Melbourne airport.

Everything you have loved
I have loved too.

for Harry

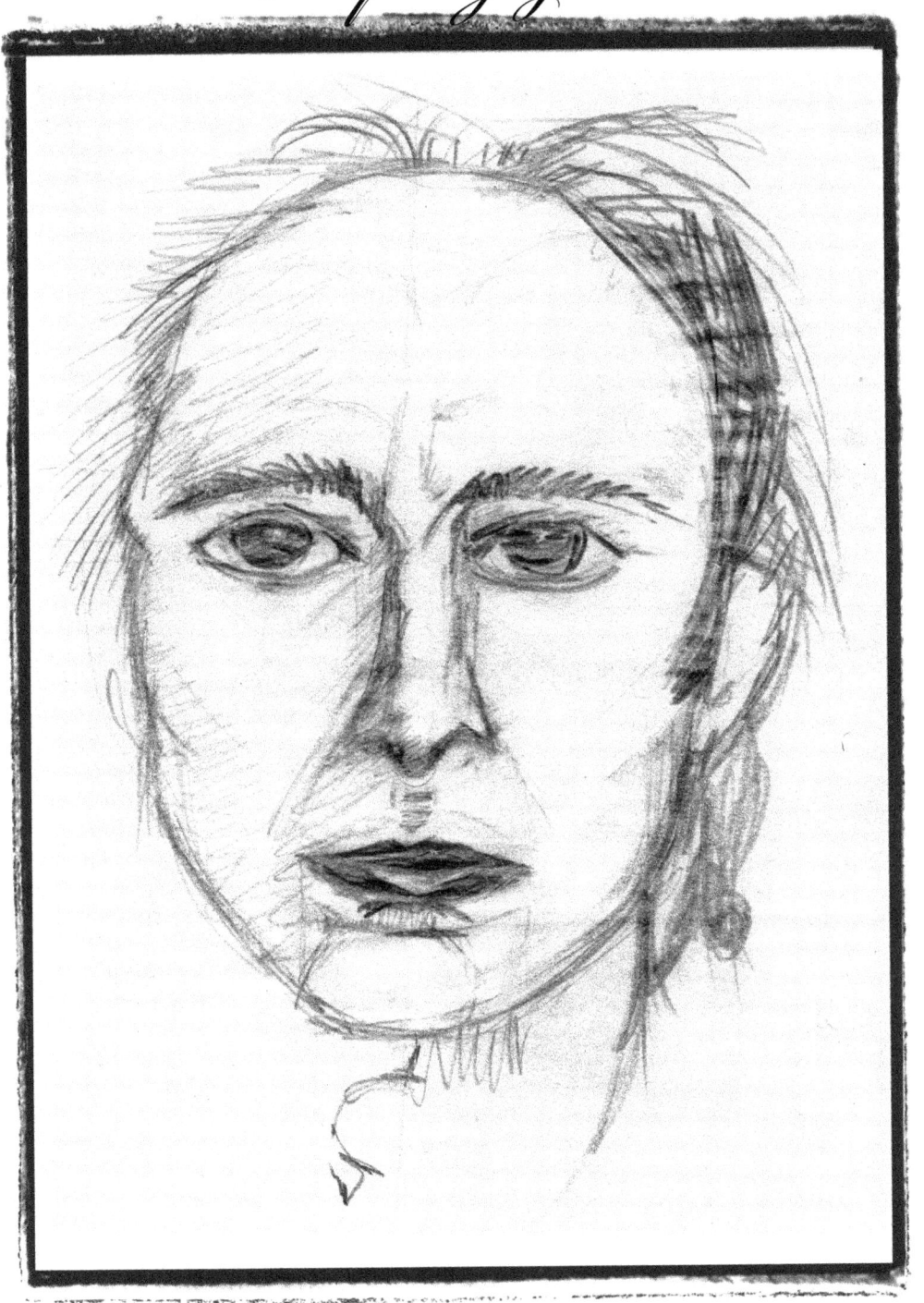

She freed me.

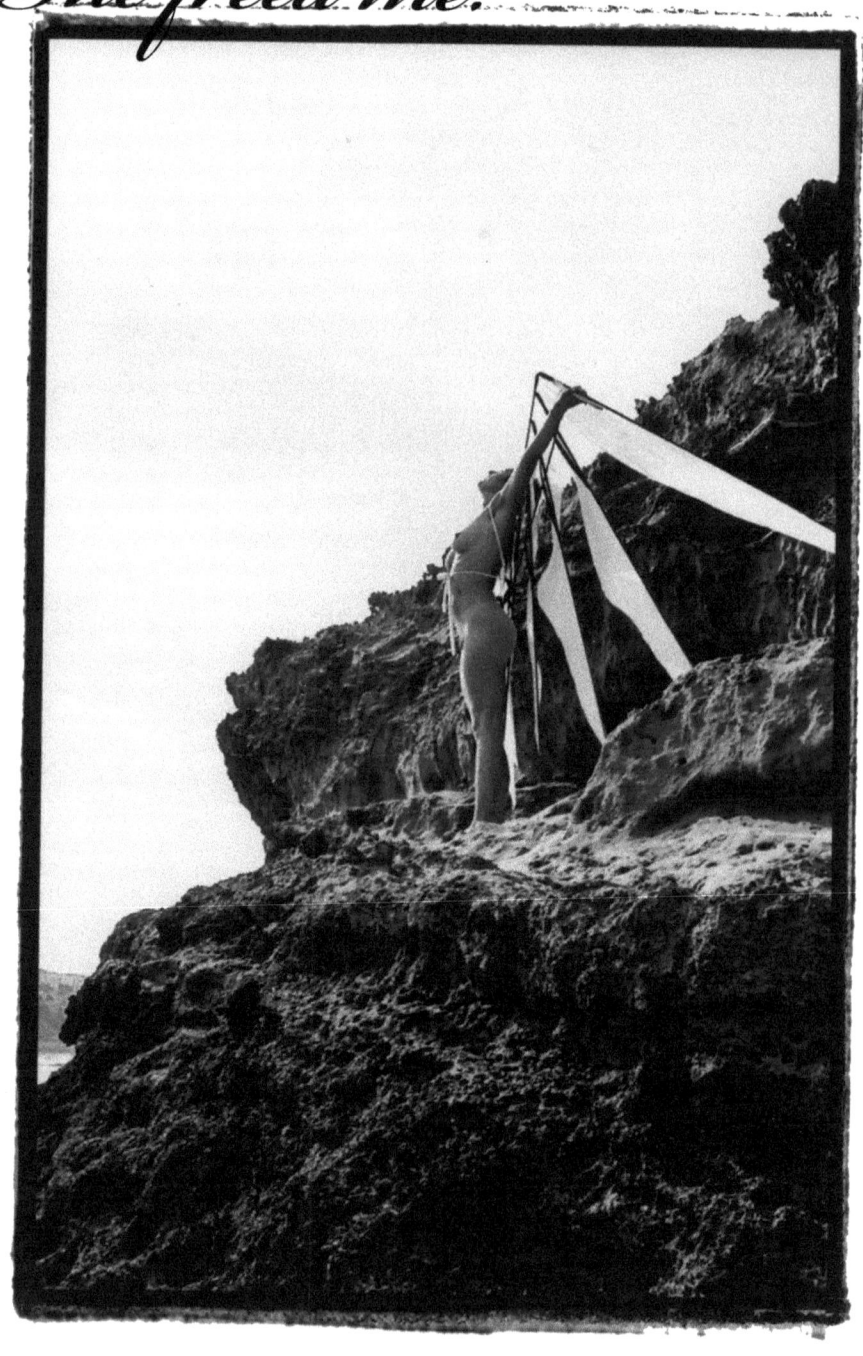

She Freed Me.

we made towers of language
so high
I fell off them
in lucid dreams

deep inside of me
a soul
twenty two years

we sheltered in these words

made a psychic haven
in beach sand with wings

in the darkness
these words scrawled fast
as swift as ripples
drawn with a single finger
in water

black ink
like the still depths
under an iceshelf
all murky and steel blue

these words
a child's
first tentative step

the first breath
of birth
gulped

a virgin girl
with fresh
nerves
sliced
like apples
from a single
touch

Jessie
radiant as the moonlight on a scribbly gum's
creamy white bark

she freed me

when she freed herself.

the found objects of love.

they were simple things
the found objects of love
notes hidden
in shells
scribbled on stones

shepherd's eyes and rough skin
not shallow hearts
we

he reminded me of all the things
the mountains, moors and estuary
steep cliffs with beach tides we had to outrun

I wanted the island of my childhood
the lilting accents of brewery men
thatchers with straw meadows
yellow as a golden delicious

a sea so rugged
you felt
shy
just looking at it

I wanted these things
they were the stuff
of dreams dug deep
by Devon's memory

etched in my soul is this nature
kept in memory's treasure chest
the whispers of apple blossom in May
the brown bare backs of horses.

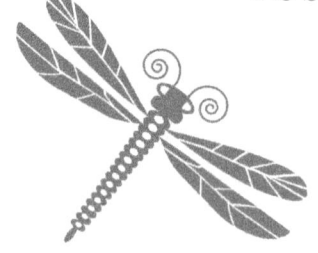

for Joe T.

the found objects of love.

The first of firsts...

It's the first of firsts for me
wrapped in black wool, possum fur and leather boots...
I am sitting at my cafe poet post
french chairs, rose paintings as big as walls, all orange and pink...
chandeliers and old masters on the ceiling

the thing of beauty that changes everything?
the light

as it ebbs and flows through the cafe window this early morning
it catches the thick candelabra and the old regal wooden chairs that
sit face to face, mind to mind, heart to heart with french striped cushions

the thing of being human that changes everything?
the heart

I cannot imagine me as only a mind...
last night I lay, exhausted from a day of work, on my bed of purple mohair
warmth
and felt my heart
soft
warm
full
and delicate

that heart that tells me oh so quietly and not everyday
"I love you"

It is that slightly imperceptible resonance in the heart chamber
that tells me I am more than the words of the
rambling
mind
plagued with doubts
questioning
analysing and fear

I am made of more than thoughts
although I use thoughts to tell you this
when that heart resonance purrs
like a sleepy warm cat
curled in a chair
the light
in the heart
is the warmth in my mother's hand
a blessing of
being alive.

Pheast48 – 1st residency morning.
6.7.2010

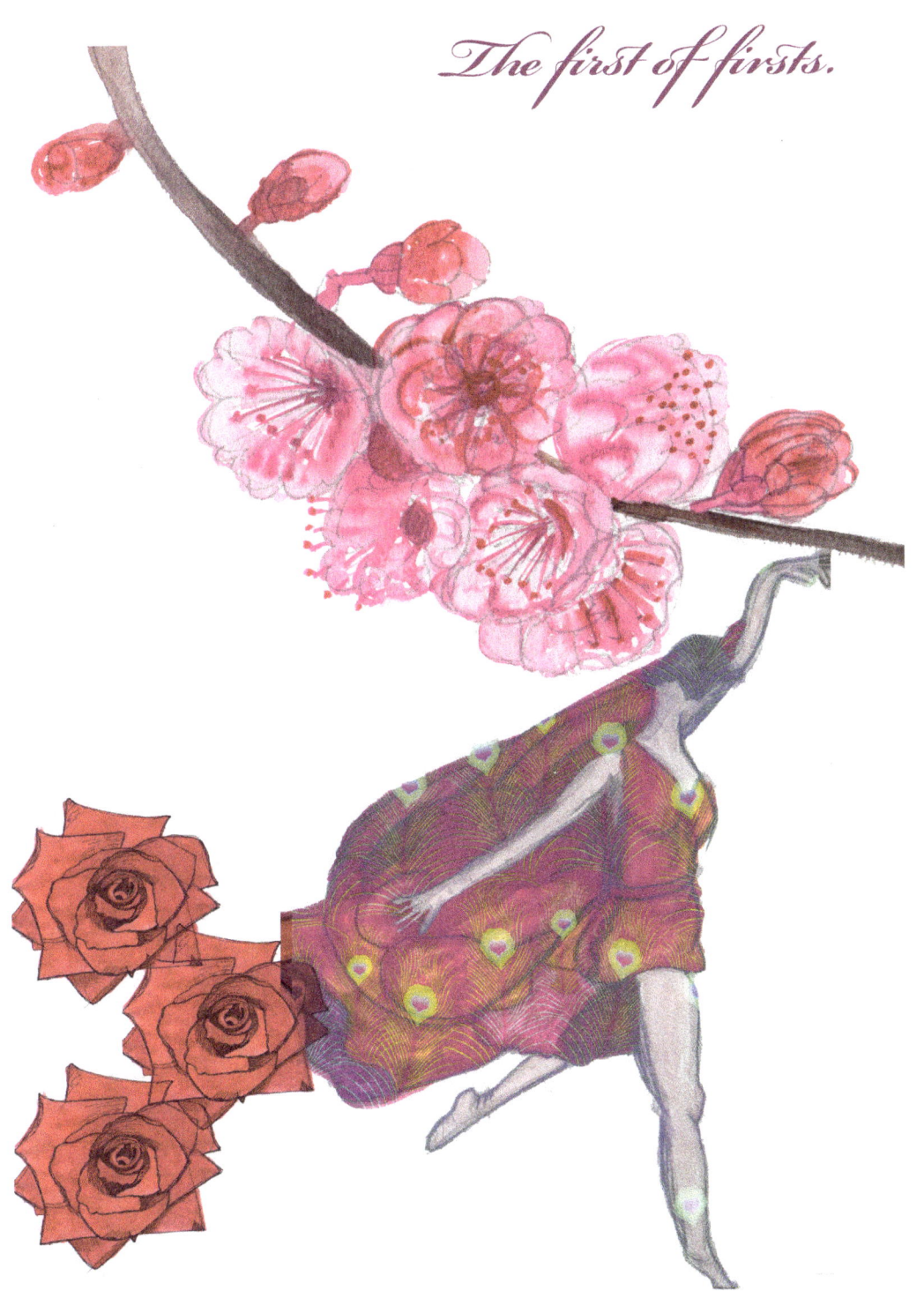

Good People.

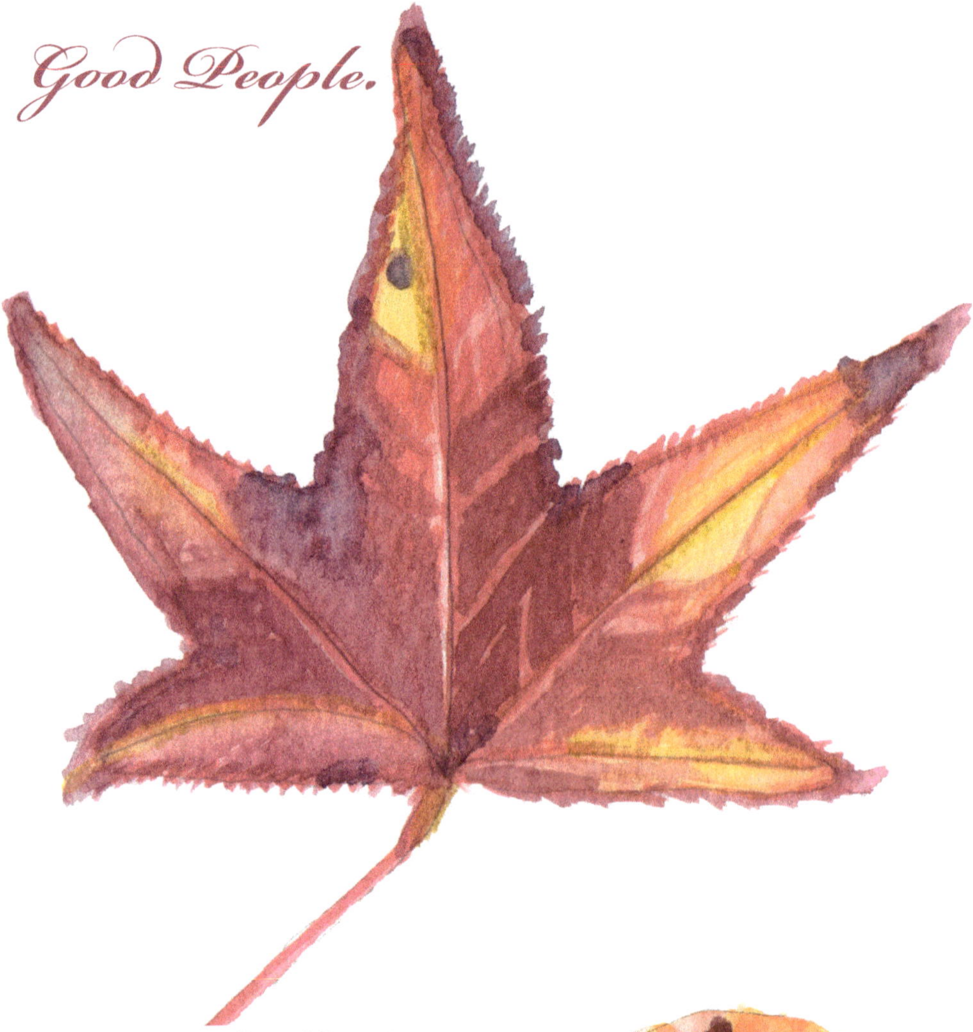

Good People.

in him is all the history
of good people

in his eyes is the theory
of attraction
personified

when the heart quickens
the race of blood
pushes the dilating pupils
into wishes and dreams.

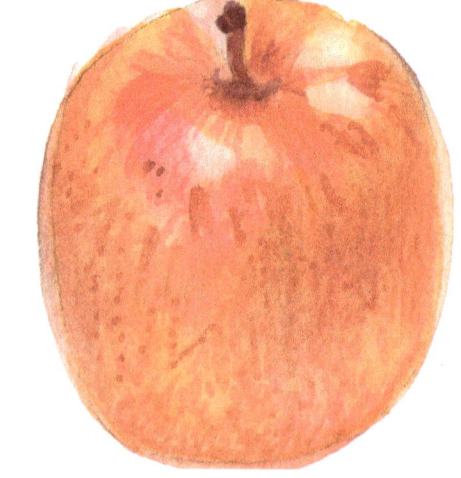

Old Man Banksia.

Old man banksia's in my blood
And he knows this man
Is seldom found
In online chat rooms
Fast and furious sex in toilets
At the latest vodka bar

Old man banksia's is in my blood
And he knows my love
Loves another
I was too late
And found myself shuffling to work
Despite the urge to pull, pull the cords tighter
So we could be together
Elsewhere
Somewhere
Other than in my head
Between the two sides of my scull
Between the cortex and the frontal lobe.

(Shit, it's a love poem and I'm mentioning frontal lobes!!!!!!)

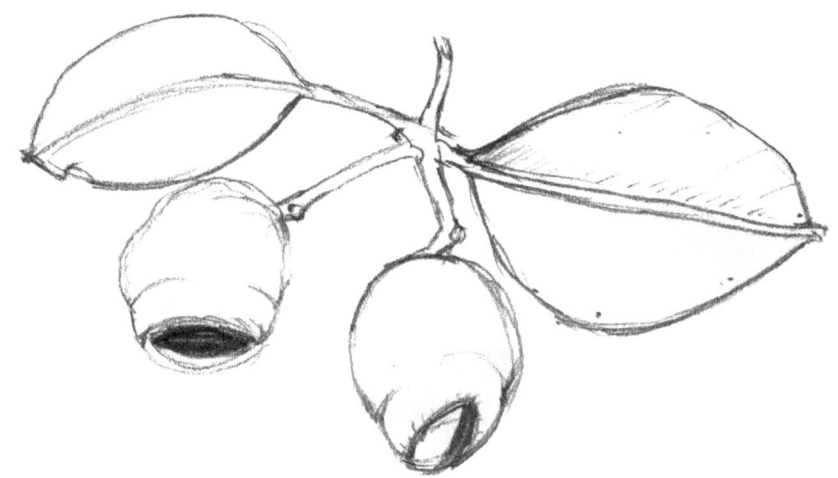

Sunflower girl.

I saw your face radiate with the light of spirit
it shone down on me in a sunflower
floating softly into my heart
petal by petal
while I lay in a padded cell

your beauty, strength and quiet faith
are gifts
when you touch me with your eyes
they say
"lie back, surrender to the earth's currents
feel your heritage, your life force"

between us are shared stories
words, always words
we talk of family, love, art

sunflower girl
the essence
of beauty both
inside and out

your spirit carries me
when all have been forgotten
and passed away

our friendship sustains
as the world sustains
as we have form
as we have spirit
our friendship nourishes.

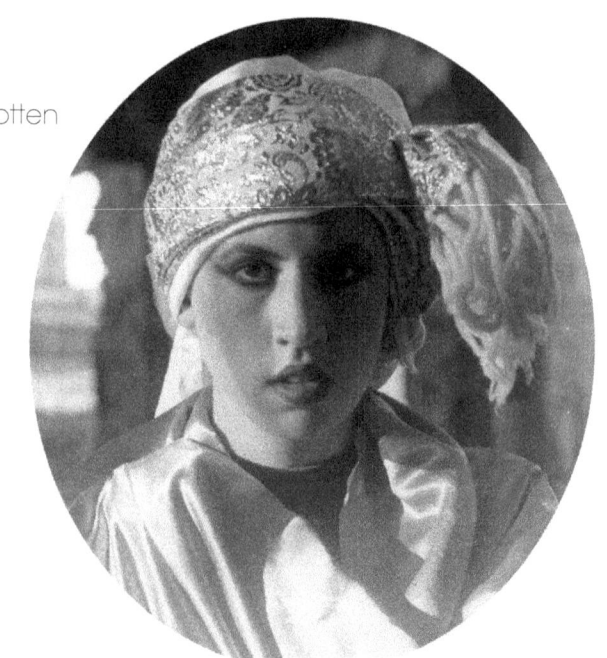

for Charlotte

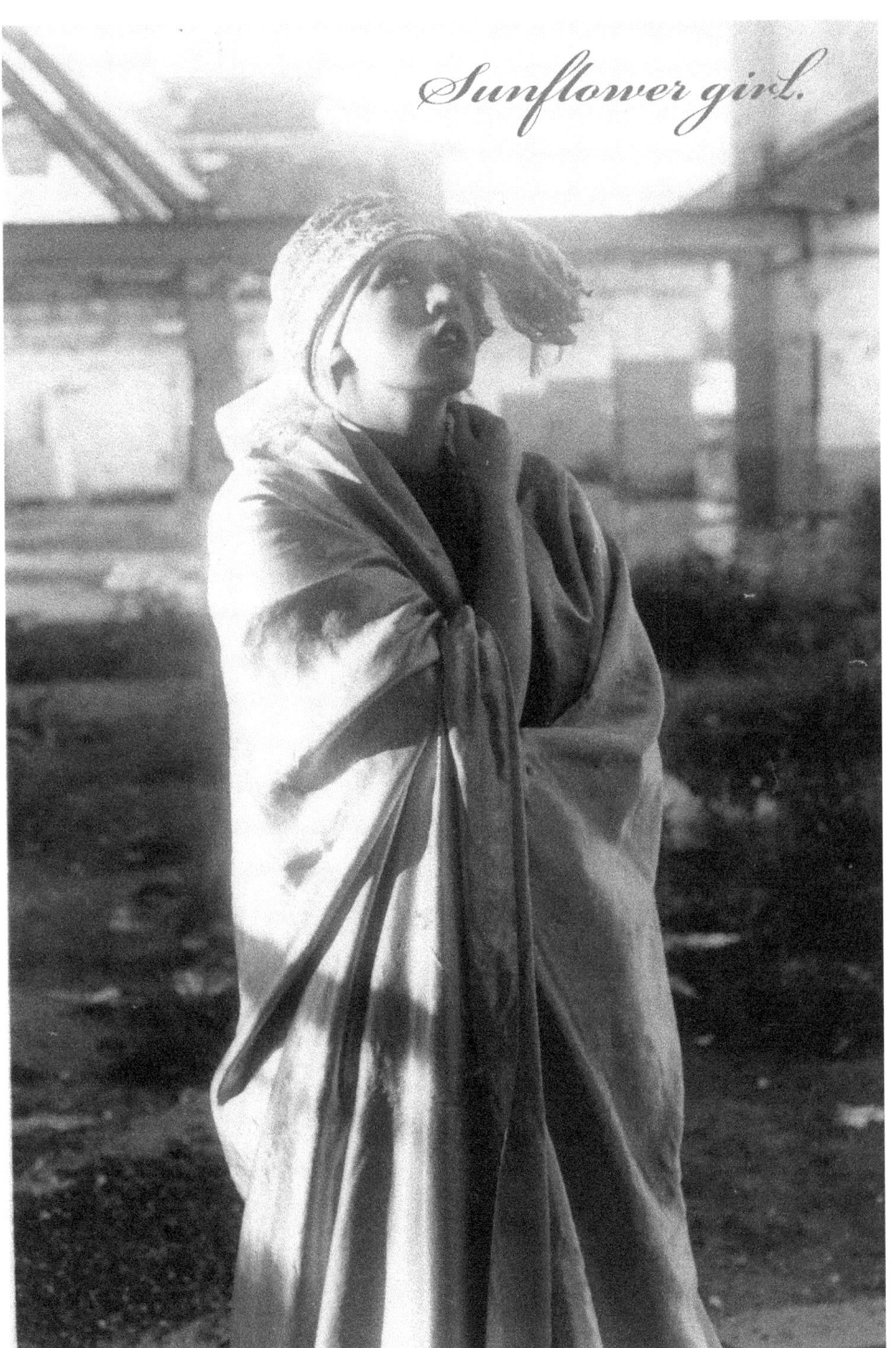

Sunflower girl.

Shadows of my Neighbourhood.

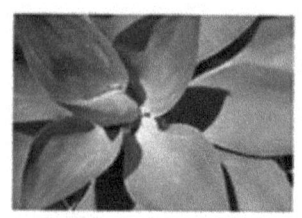

Each new day
I haunt
the grassy avenues and crescents
of this
my neighbourhood

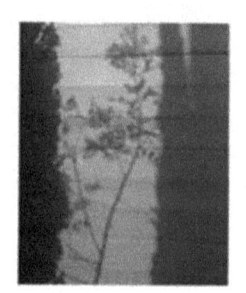

My dog and I
walk the streets
the green tree-lined courts and lanes

We telepathise
as her silky black back
sways and sashays around the alleys

Sometimes my fight with the
invisible milkbar
and its infamous 70% cocoa chocolate bar
is won and I powerwalk home

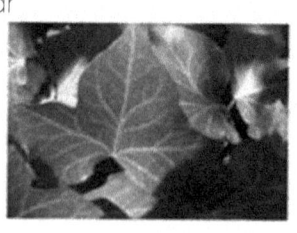

Though sometimes I lose this fight
and I walk an hour
working off
the cashew nut baklava from Divine Deli

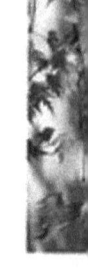

I'm standing in the shadows
of my neighbourhood
seeking community
but instead
finding
communion

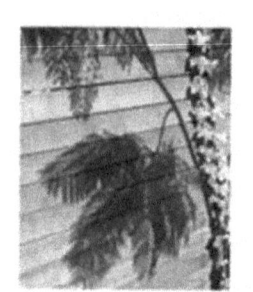

The birds
I see blackbirds and myna
I hear turtle dove and sparrow
in my imagination
I touch, 'Oh so small!'
with the velvety warm hand
tucked in my boiled black wool coat

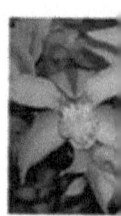

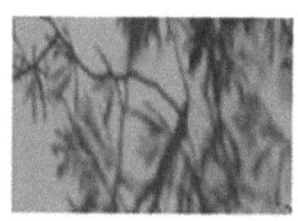

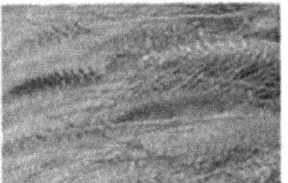

Shadows of my Neighbourhood.

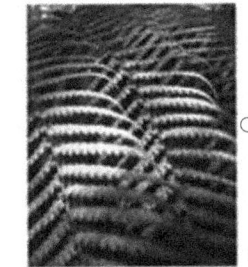

"Look, look!" I say to Zula
as we notice the squawking songs of king parrots
just down from the bush for a few days
in this fruit season

Rosellas in my favourite tree
a native gum with bleached grey green bark
and pink dancing blossoms

Up close I devour the delicate detail
and deliciousness for the honey-eater beak

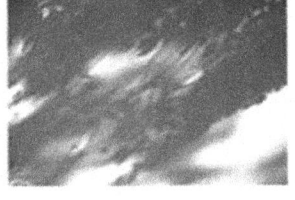

I am mesmerised by the buzz and excitement of the birds
and shocked when a
raven eyes me
from a mere foot away

But I am home

In a moment

I am home

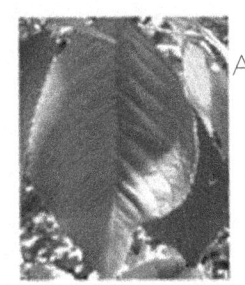

A lonely man, himself and his dog nearly blind
seeks this neighbour's connectionI
am happy to oblige for a time
but seek sanctuary
in quiet afternoons
in deserted family streets

I am no risk taker
but love these daily suburban adventures
wandering finds a momentary home
in time I hope to belong.

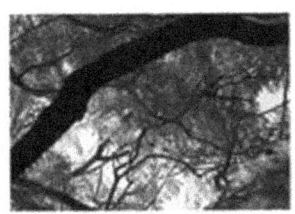

Living Between the Worlds.

some
like our birds
live between sky and sea

some
like our trees
breathe between soil and heaven

but
I live
between earth and ether

my days
are conversations
with the dead

my nights
are delirious and haunted
both

living between the worlds
where truth
I am told
is holy

my days are situations
I can't control
even inside my mind.

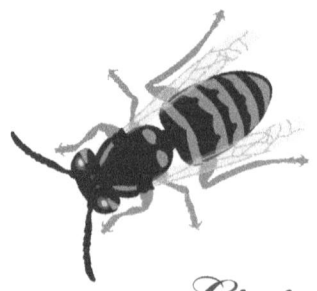

Living Between the Worlds.

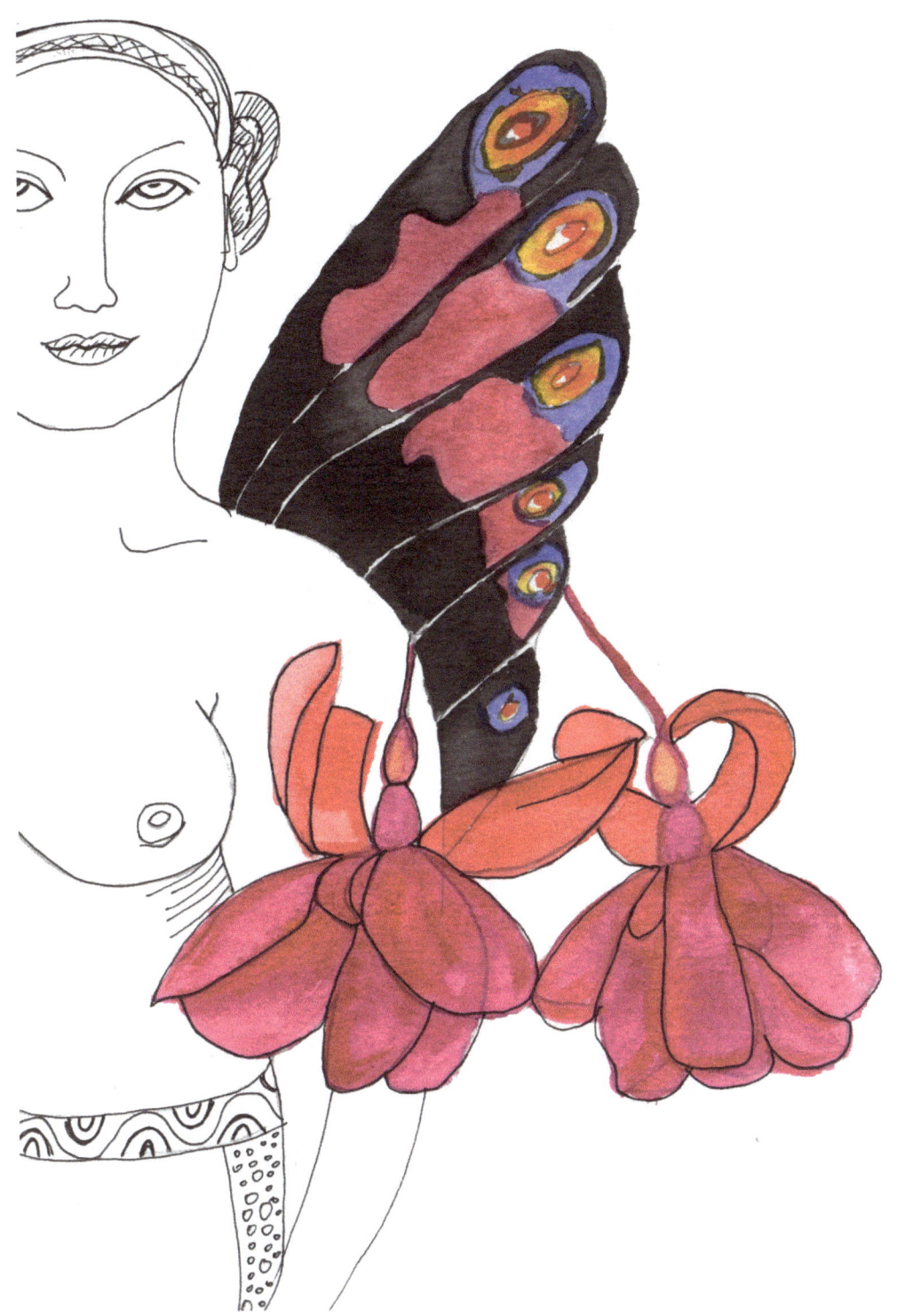

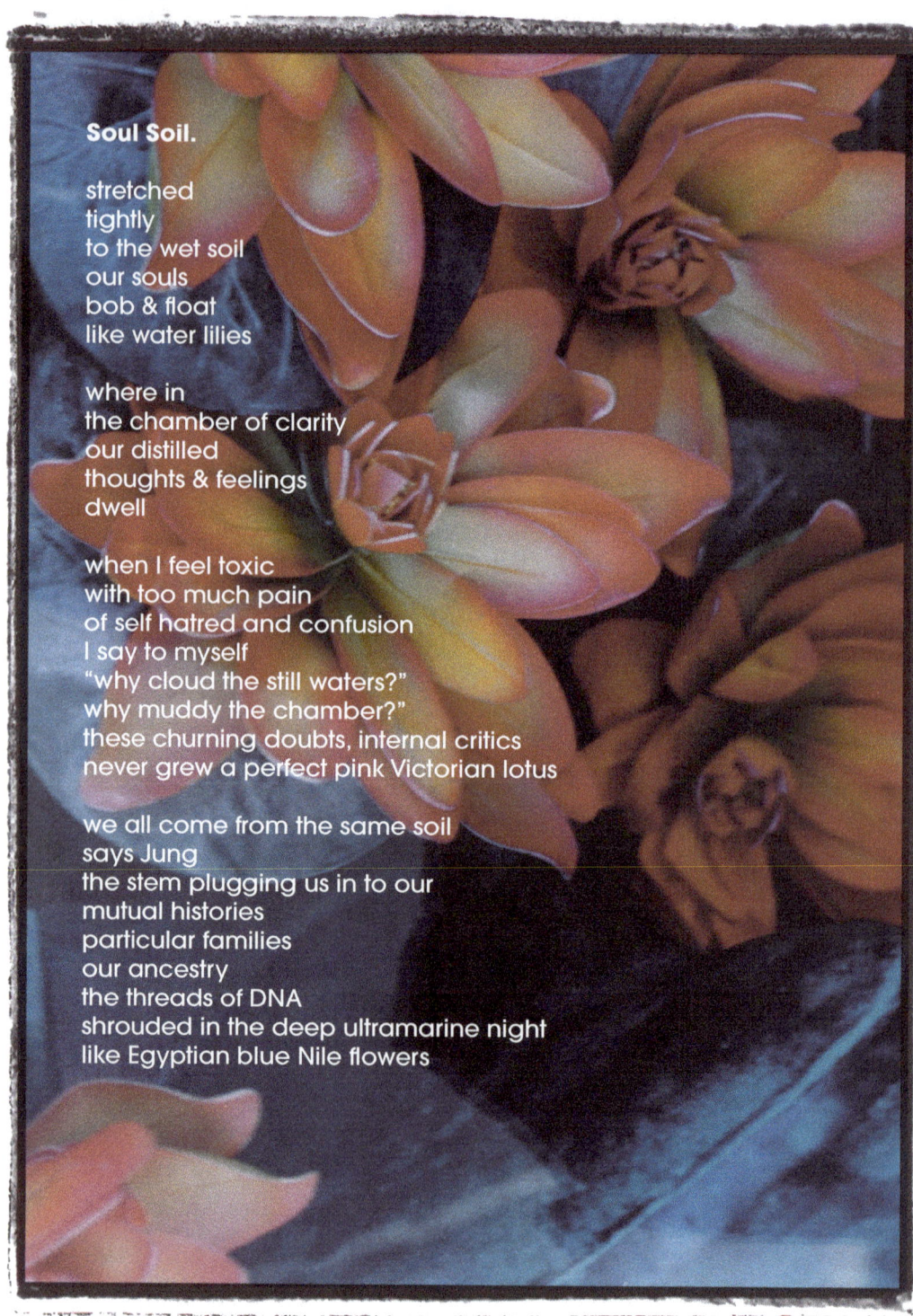

Soul Soil.

stretched
tightly
to the wet soil
our souls
bob & float
like water lilies

where in
the chamber of clarity
our distilled
thoughts & feelings
dwell

when I feel toxic
with too much pain
of self hatred and confusion
I say to myself
"why cloud the still waters?"
why muddy the chamber?"
these churning doubts, internal critics
never grew a perfect pink Victorian lotus

we all come from the same soil
says Jung
the stem plugging us in to our
mutual histories
particular families
our ancestry
the threads of DNA
shrouded in the deep ultramarine night
like Egyptian blue Nile flowers

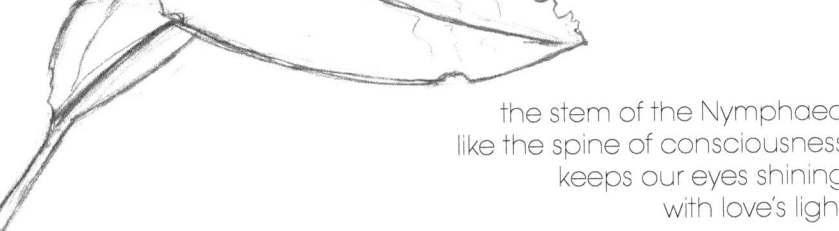

the stem of the Nymphaea
like the spine of consciousness
keeps our eyes shining
with love's light

the soil is our
collective conscious
our togetherness
bound by millennia
crawling from the sea
into low branches of
genealogy trees
to lull infront of TVs
the journey from source
our roots untangling
into single stems

with our heads bowed
gentle words flow
we cherish the soil
that made it so.

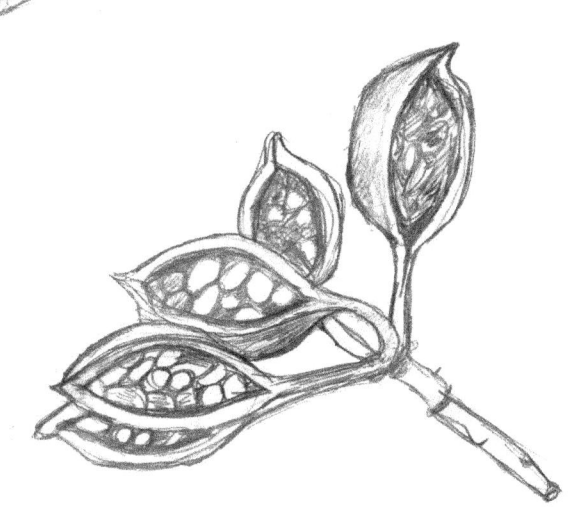

Soul Soil.

We are mother and child.

Tucked in her dreamy peachy body
on her knee that supports and holds
a blessed place of warmth
the curves
squishy bits
firm embrace of my mother
the landscapes explored over and over
swishing down the knees
like a slide
a million miles long

I instinctively know
her every scent
touch of hair
flavour of skin
closeness of breath
the breath shared between
mouths
wide smiling mouths
where the river of energy
from one to the other
can be distinguished from all

we are mother and child.

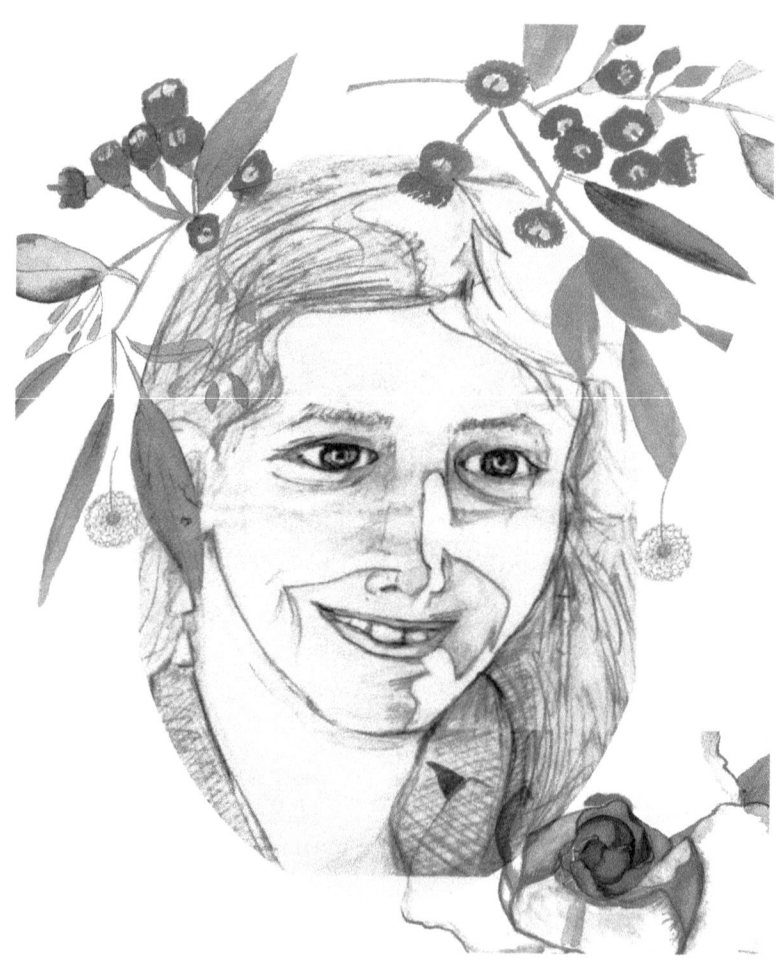

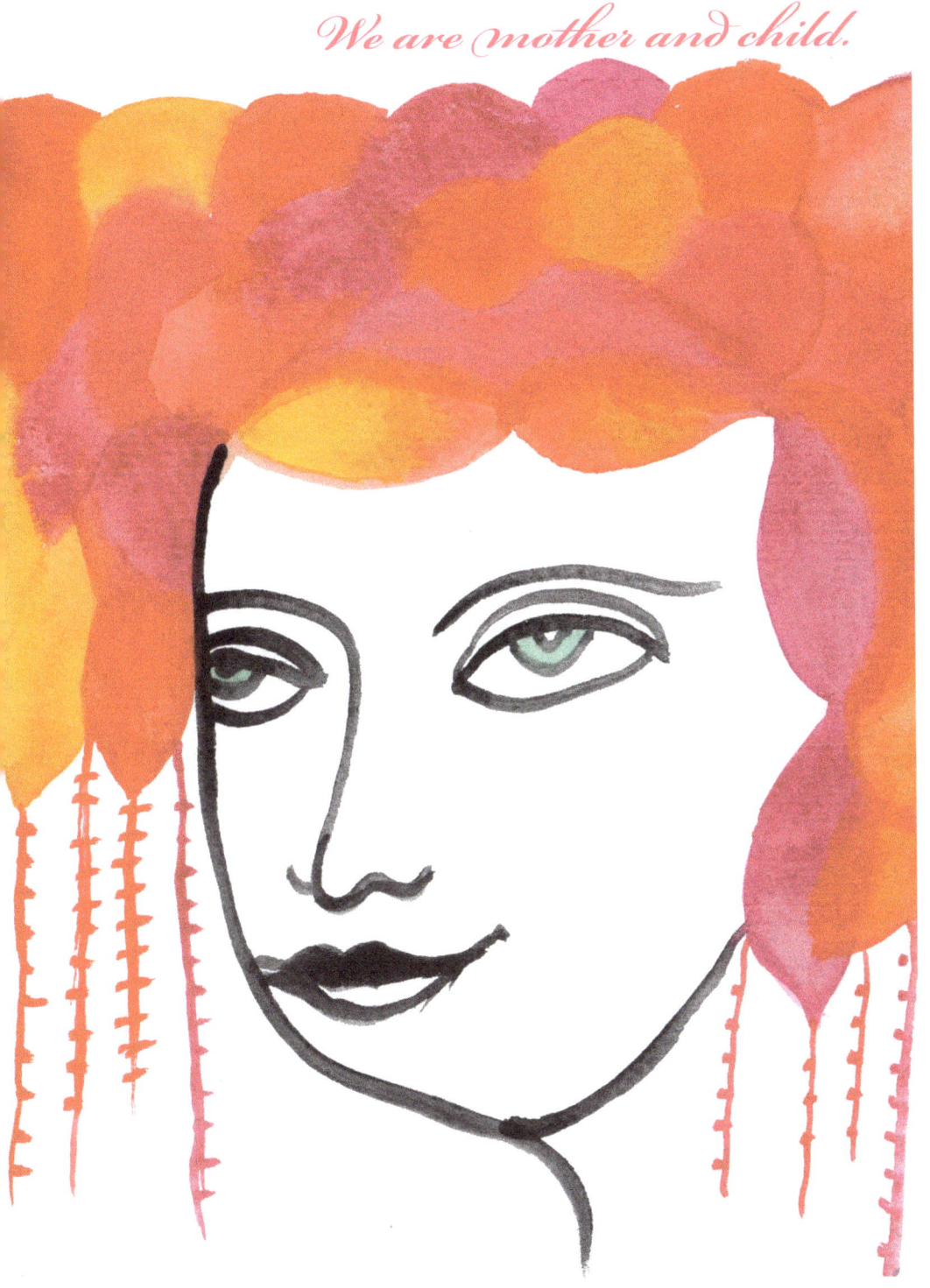

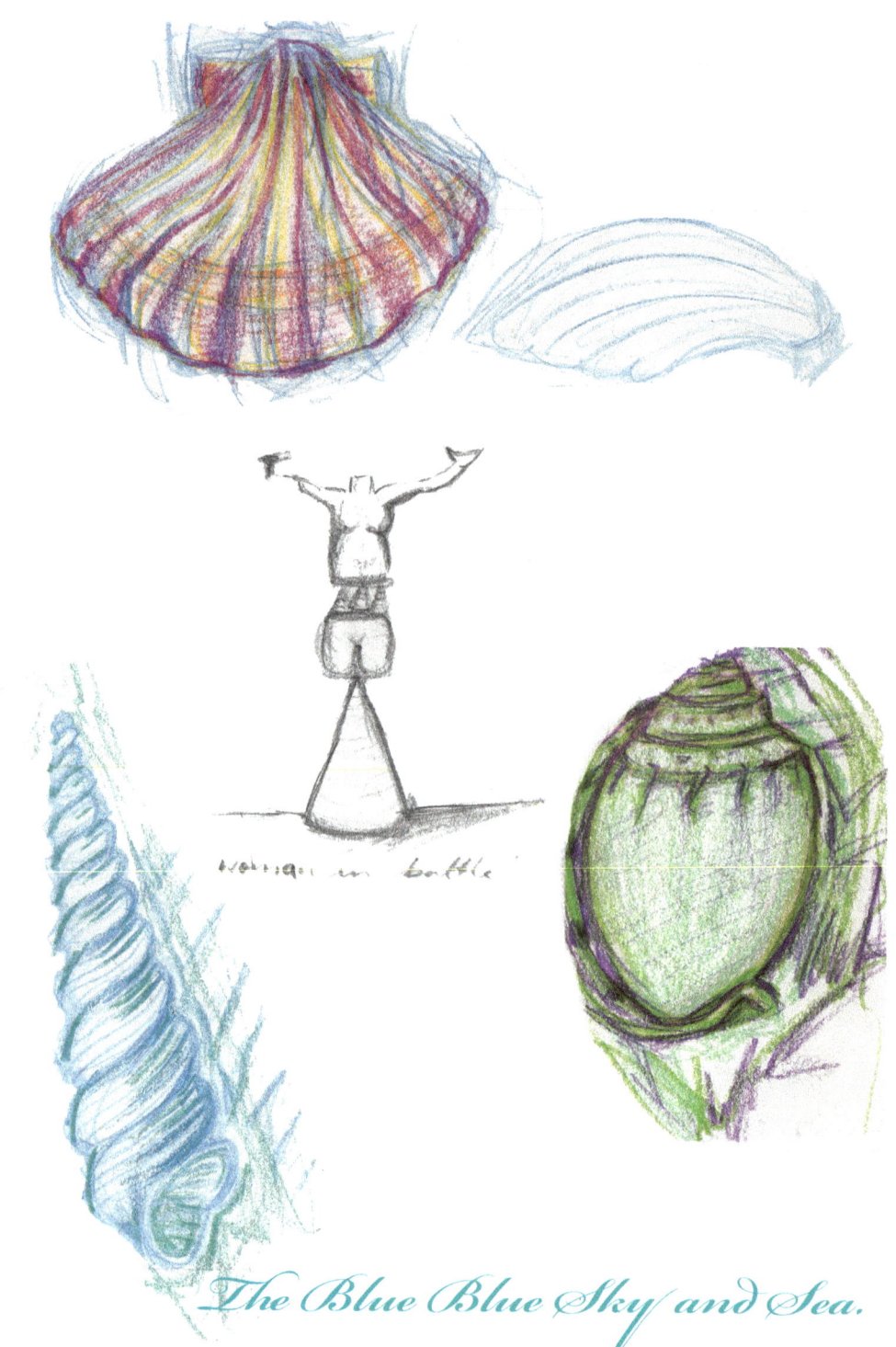

woman in bottle

The Blue Blue Sky and Sea.

42

The Blue Blue Sky and Sea.

The blue blue sky and sea
the expanse that sustains us
Australia.
It is like our very lifeblood

While here we drift on days of turquoise seas and clear skies
this country stimulates the currents of newness
to skirt and duck the conflicts of mighty nations
and no longer struggle when it is free

We carry each other
in the folds of our arms
we carry each other again, again and again
each time it gets longer
each time the lessons press
deeper and deeper
into our palms

I am weary of this fight
this fighting to find a place

On days, it seems our land
is scolded for her unruliness
borders indistinct
townships appear spoiled
left to abandon in the hot sun
their weathered sides leach out
rusty paint from corrugated roofs

a land of fierce beauty
incomparable delicate ecology
innumerable unique species
within the blue blue sky and sea
of expanses that nourishes us
Australia.

Nature – a gift.

eating doughy-sweet gugelhupf
at Monarch cafe
where echoes of migrant Italian culture
soothe against abrasive echo chambers
all steel and concrete

leaving the studio
my paradise
choking fumes from the
eight-lane highway
assault me
as the wind drives its hectic hands into
my warm centre
while
monster metal buses
burp toxic smoke

all is devoid of beauty
where are Nature's lullabies?
soothing me in joyous colour
the only tool this artist needs

urine and rubbish
drains and barbed wire
the daily grime
of man-made life
coats my skin with filth
and the ghosts of generations past
scurry in fear
of modernity

I am not here by choice
am I?
are you?

when did culture with a capital
become defined
by chaos and meanness?
the New World clash of the
potent
yet
pointless
acquiring of money

I am not your billboard
I am not your next big thing

I am living between worlds
where Nature is the
only true Intelligence
and we fit in there somewhere
although we have forgotten
our place.

it is my plea we remember
nature
is a gift.

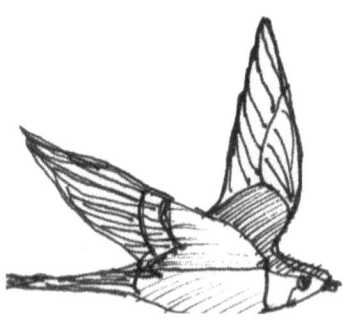

44

Nature - a gift.

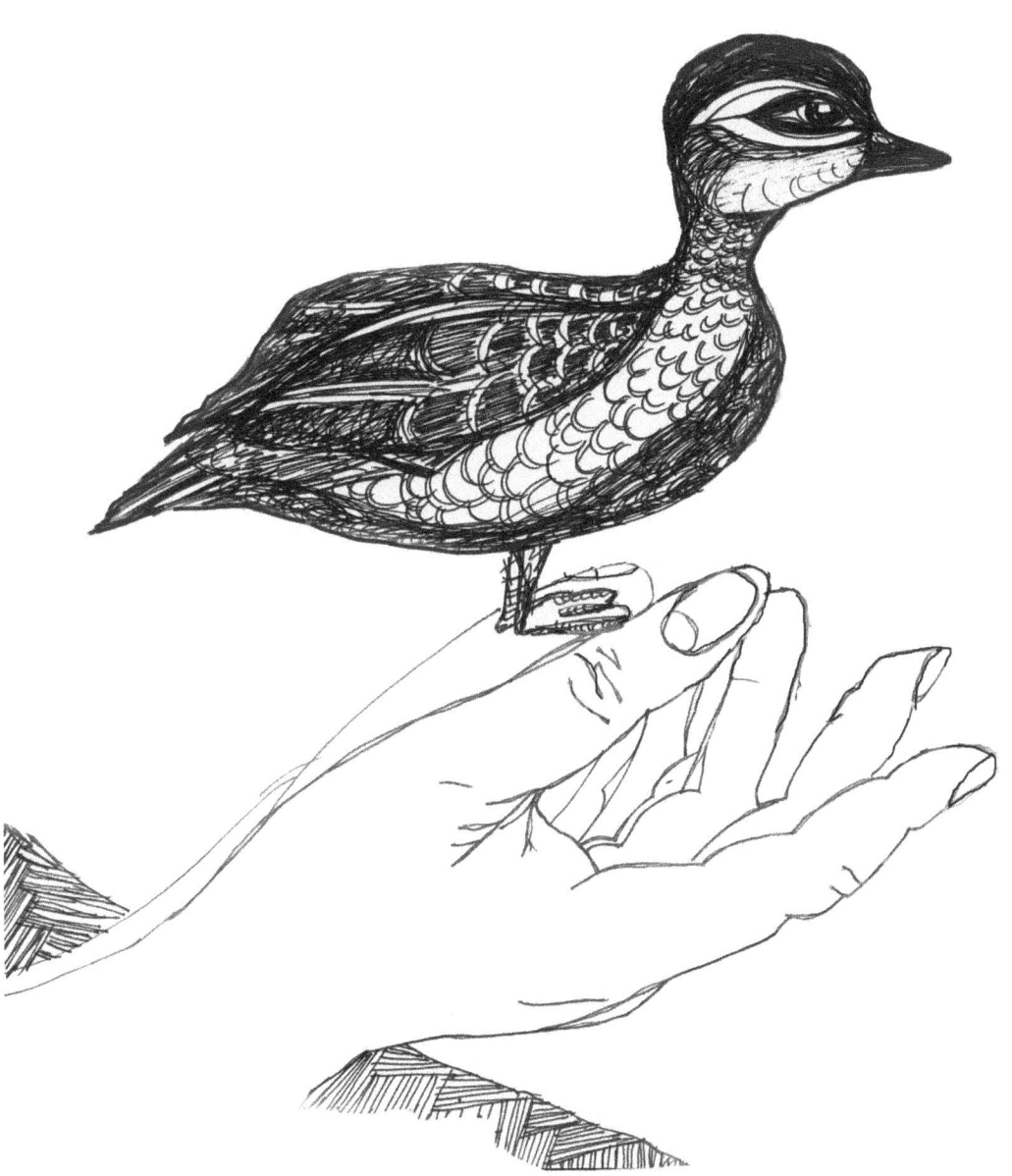

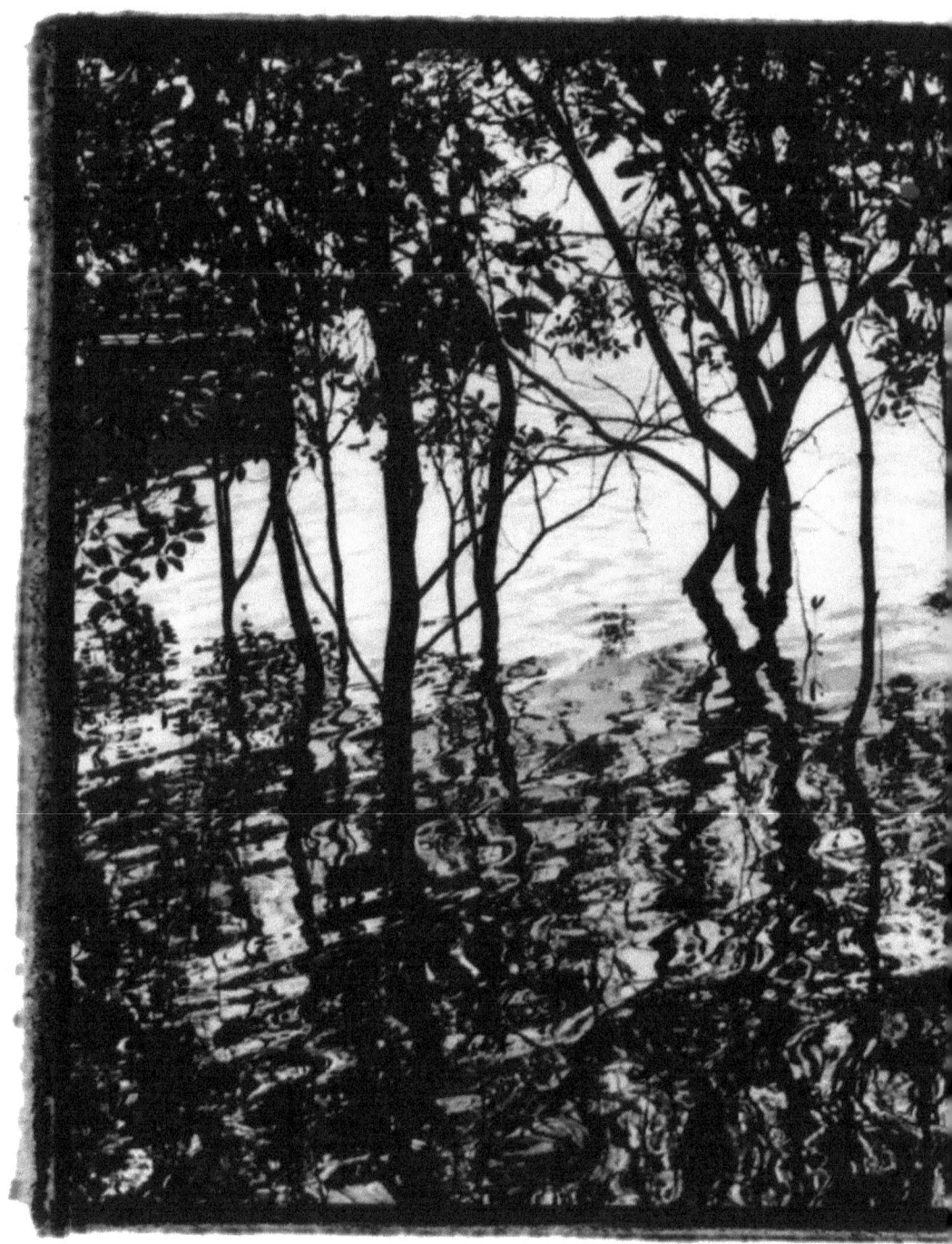

Dying Man.

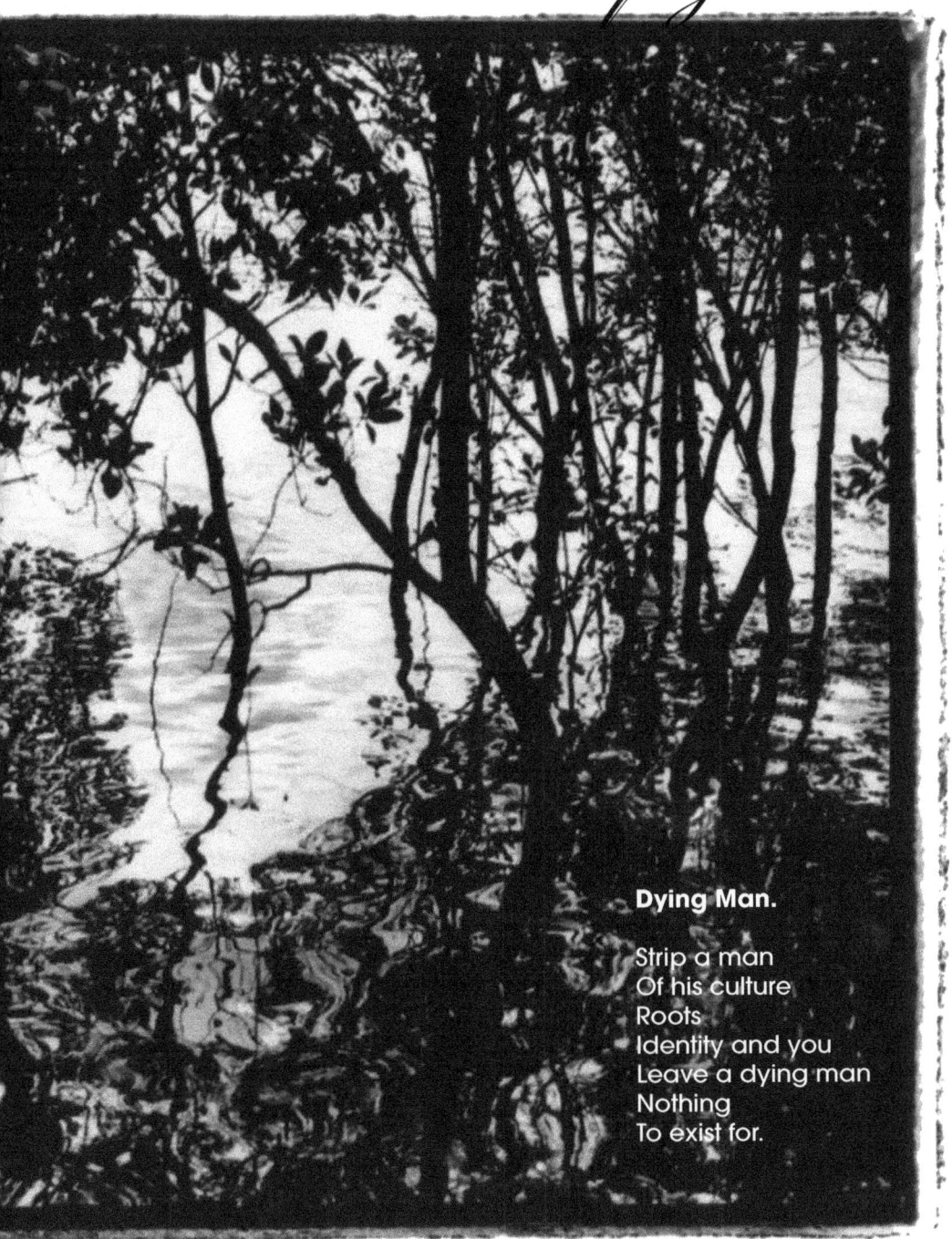

Dying Man.

Strip a man
Of his culture
Roots
Identity and you
Leave a dying man
Nothing
To exist for.

Older Brother.

I've got O.B.S
'older brother syndrome'
the elder of siblings unmatchable
in kindness, intelligence and gifts
of music, art and poetry
the one that went first
to travel over the oceans
a brother whose warmth
can melt my invisible devil tattoos

held in his compassionate glance
like that of a master, aura transparent
whose single wish is to hold
his daughter Lucy safe.

for Tali

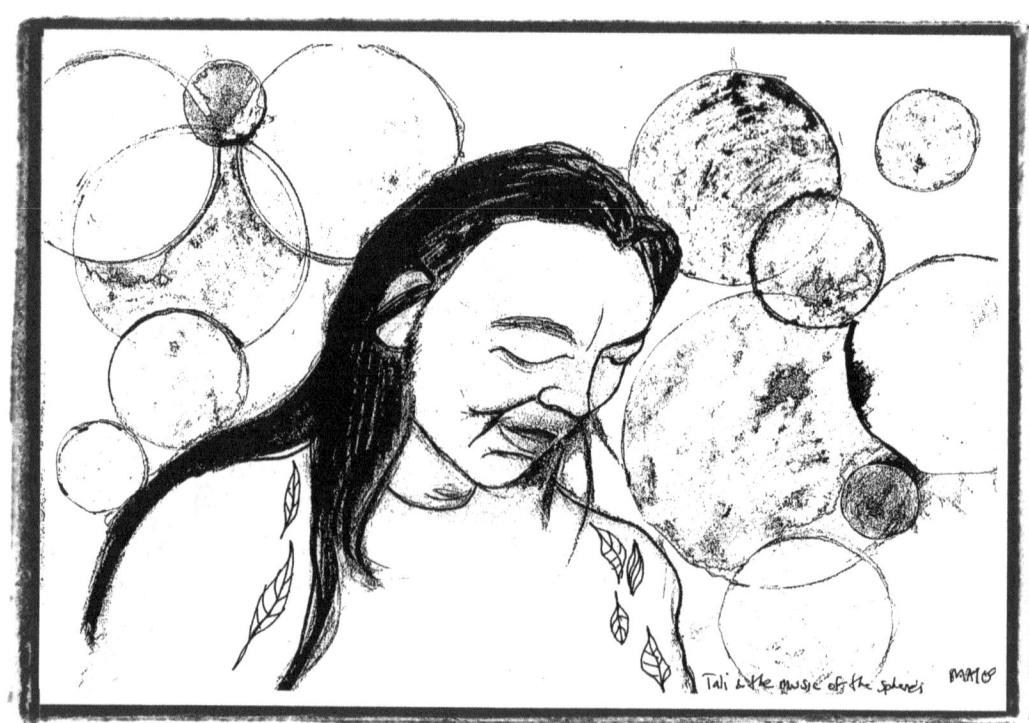

Tali like music of the spheres

Darkest Regrets.

I walked the streets, cold and alone
with no hope or friends or money
I walked the streets, almost, to abase myself
to the darkest fears and the darkest regrets
of never having
loved
myself
in a gilded language
I tore myself to bits

I stepped off this street
into a house in Carlton whose lino loved no-one
I tried to soothe myself from shy tears
I tried to beleive in love and yet was hated
bitten by her venom I grew weak
weak and trapped in self-loathing's black mirror

I had been caught in a mesmerising life
of traffic and Turkish coffee readings with poached
eggs at three in the afternoon
I found no relief in my imagination
no reprieve in talking books accompanied
with sewing patchwork
or in student-ish poetry

I found solace in others' words
The Tibetan Book of Living and Dying
concepts that became just simple words
telling me of our common humanness
how life could be bland, could be
unexpectedly disappointing
how a social veneer could
hide the truth of life's
darkest regrets.

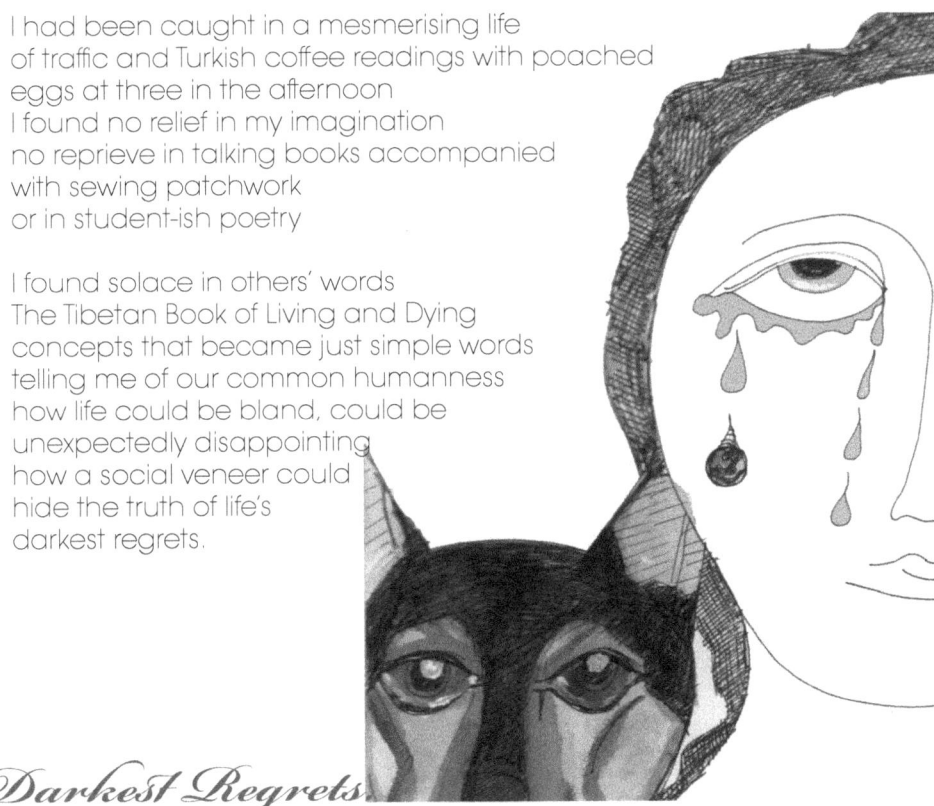

Darkest Regrets.

Faith.

Things seem to shift
silently
like beggars on the street
shuffle together
slowly towards home.
I had been wandering for a time
in this street
of no hope
no lasting happiness
no faith
lifted only by what my sight could sustain
and only at a distance

Maybe the expanse of sea and sky at dusk
maybe a horizon of hills
like Ireland's Ring of Kerry
maybe my grandfather's country
but all things move me less
now

And poetry?
poetry is a resting place
It calls me home
but only
I
can lift my hands
to pray

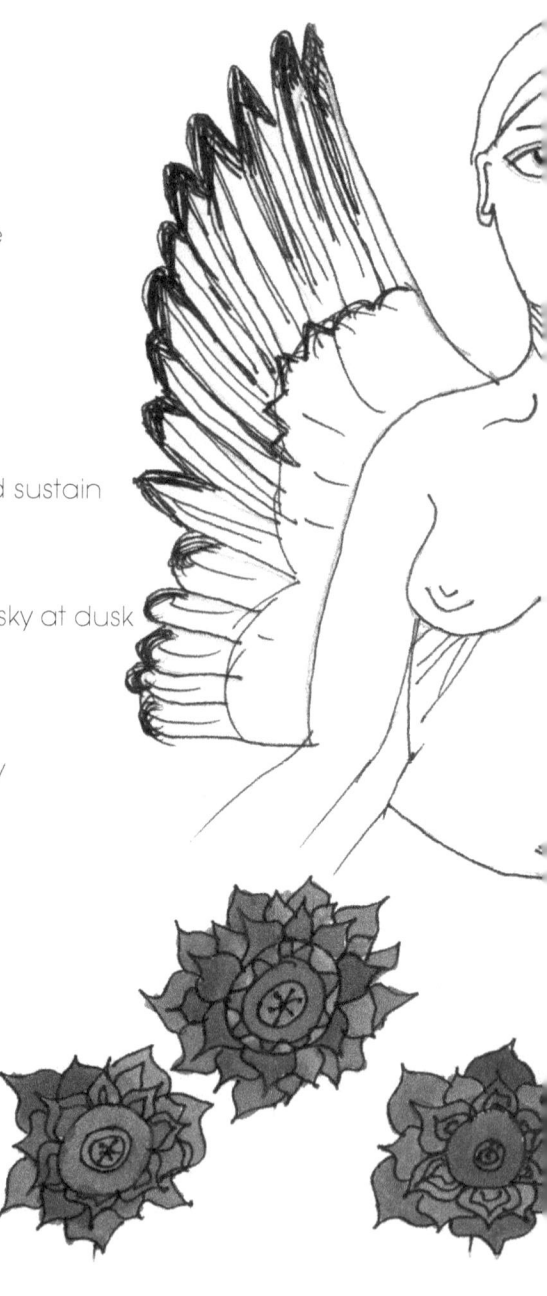

Faith.

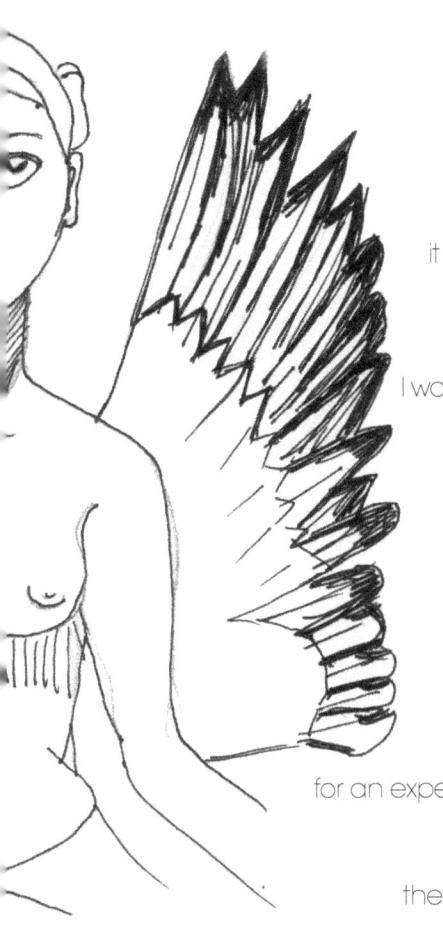

And in this moment
it seems are all the preparations of my years
spent in the dismal, dark cities of my mind.

I was naked, without the armour round my heart
And, it seems, as if I dreamt these things
many years ago
as if
I am many dreamers at once

Faith is the word
for a whole world
for an experience . . . that dictionaries cannot source.
faith
the word came to me when I had no use for it
because in my life there was a barrenness
I could not see
and
in this life
I strived.

This Ancient Land.

In the Land

That is their culture

I am visitor

No ancestors here

Flying above the ocean

The clouds

The endless blue

This ancient land

Their homeland

Generations of giving

Of stories

Of dreaming

Of language

It's beautiful.

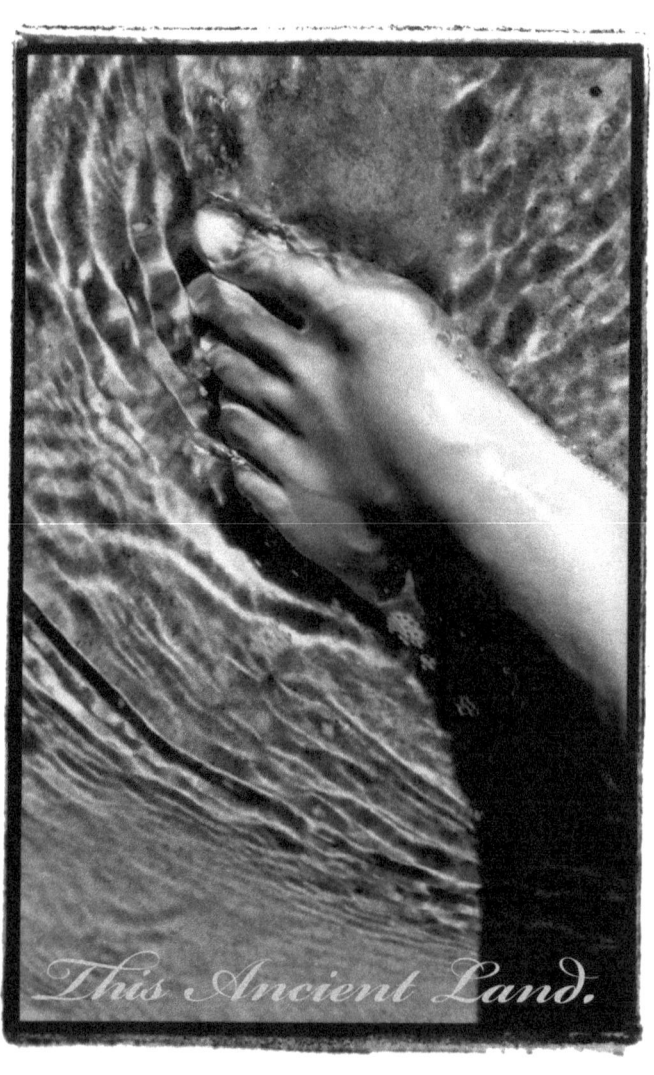

This Ancient Land.

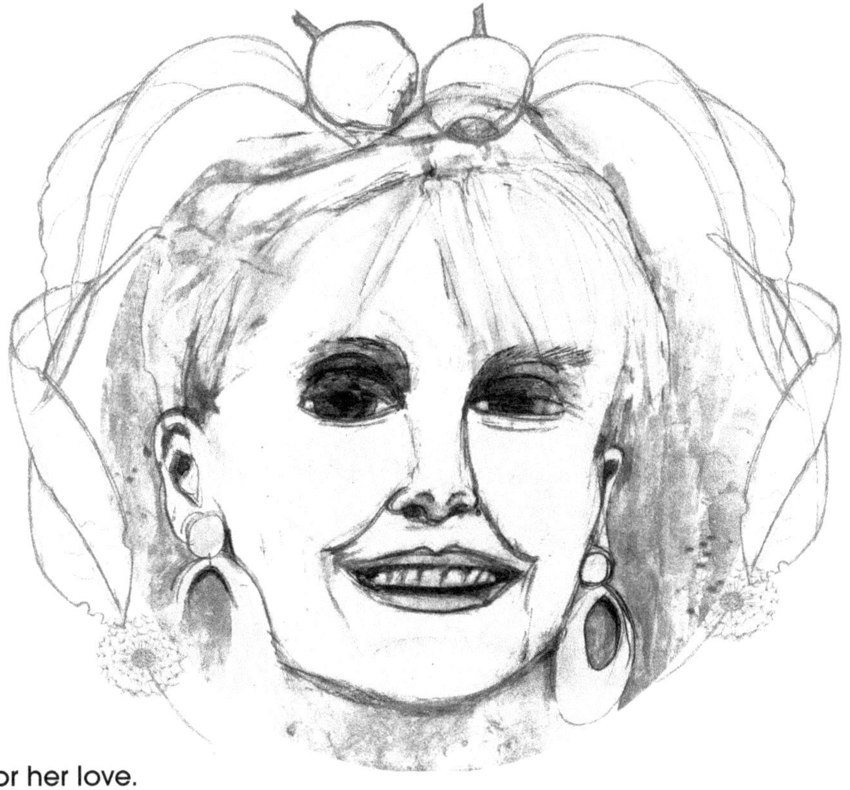

for her love.

for her love
I would do anything
to hear her words
many would swim
a bay of waters wide

in her arms
is the strength of ten
to be held in them
is to feel encircled
in a deep magenta warmth

her eyes are hazel
with the knowing and potency
of a gifted soul

I love her as she is
unique.

for Gilli

for her love.

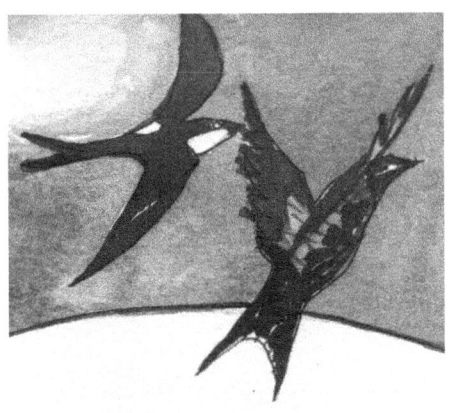

53

String.

What does it matter?
In all things passing, I am just one
And every day
a new tear

A tear of forgetting
A tear of loneliness
A tear of arriving
A tear of happiness
And in this, my "life"
all days coming and going

And I
am just another
coming and going

A dreamer
With a slow dream unravelled
Only to be wound up again
By some new plan or
action

Who is the unraveller?
And who is unravelled?

This, I am not sure, but it is certain
I am not the small "I"
I am not the beholder of life
I am merely the beheld

Like a flower
I am held within the grasp of God
I can be crushed!
Please, oh! please let me be crushed
So, I am the raw scent
raw goodness
alive in stillness

I want to feel all life leave me
to be an empty vessel
I want to lie at the feet of the Buddha,
God, the Immortal Power beyond Duality
And to lie and be as the flower
Cut, weeping at the stem
I feel as if I have been severed
weeping is the time spent away

But, I have found my way home through the forest of thought
A heavy, burdensome mind
Heavy with I's and We's and When's

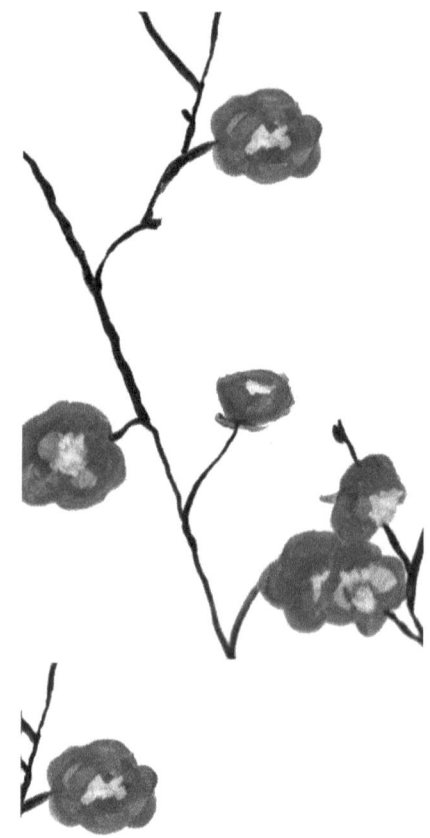

I am weary of the effort
I am weary of being just one

How is is that there are so many of us, God?
Why are you so close, yet unreachable?
How did I not see you before?
How was it that the sky was so obscured by such a small droplet of rain?

Can you clear the clouds one day, entirely?
Why do I have to walk in this world without you?
You are like the best mind, clear of all thinking, full of suggestion

String.

Oh Buddha, sometimes when I am without you
all things, all things are empty!
Nothing bears fruit
All seems barren
There are no dreamers
and no dream
and it seems as if I have wandered again
into some foreign land, and I call your name
my Beloved
and yes indeed
I see your sullen face
in all the city dwellers
beside me
on the train
on the street
on the tram

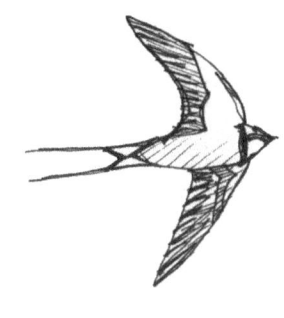

We are alive
But only with the spark
Your divine spark, which animates all things

And I am nothing
Without your wish
If my wish is not your wish
My joy not your joy
my intention not your intention
Then
I am nothing
I am lost
And all things are empty and void
My wishes cannot bear fruit
Without the seed of your love

B E E

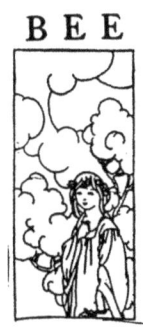

"Lo, I am always with you means
when you look for God
God is in the look of your eyes,
Nearer to you than yourself . . .
Be like melting snow,
Wash yourself of yourself."
Rumi

The light.

the light
begins as just a glint
like frozen water shards
in an Inuit's grin

from this light
we
breathe as air
drink as water
eat and digest
all we share
touch
taste
consummate

from our form
comes innocent
unnamable
beauty
that of a child

a child whose eyes shine
twinkle in merriment
like old men in pubs
with chips and condiments

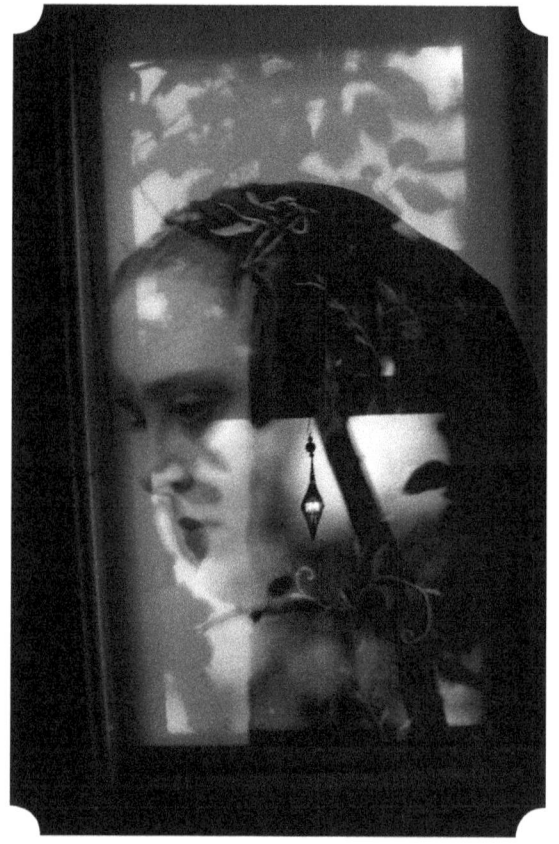

denser and denser forms
of incarnated source
the essence of us, alive
a light on fire
in the deep azure blue centre
pulsing beneath the skin

without the light
darkness would descend
the sun swallowed by ravens
eternally frozen
in perpetual night
my primal fear

the photosynthesis of leaves
captured and stored sunlight
within golden filigree viens

our breath
trees' next breath
the soil
their nurturance
our sustenance

fruit harvest of nourishment
lemons in winter
peaches in spring
pills of Earth's making
wrapped in rind
caressed in skin
Like a wild white rose
All soft and dewy.

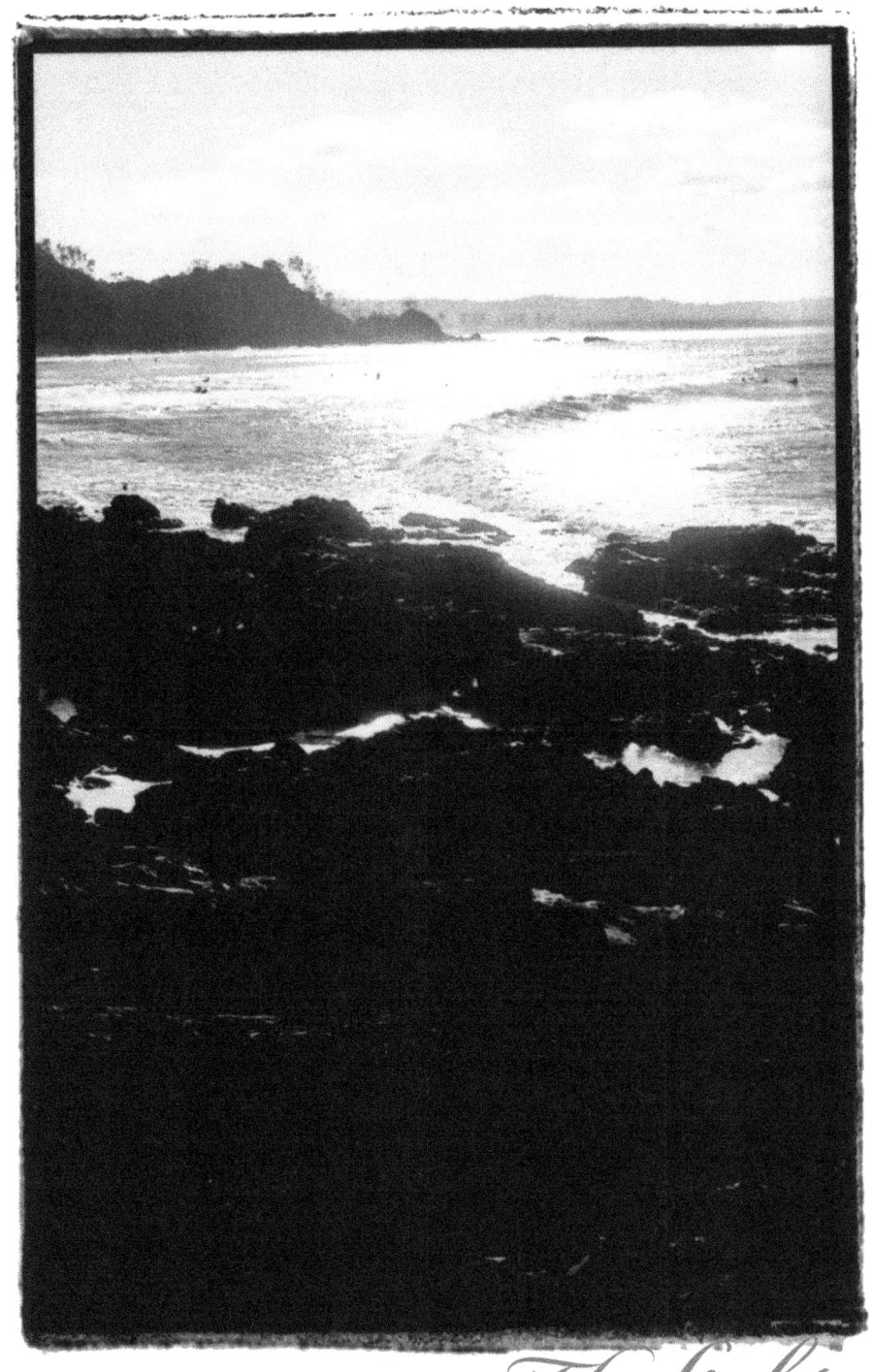

The light.

Ancient by Design.

Like Cézanne
In the forests of Provence
God paints everyday
Every detail exact
And unique

Just like you
Just like you

Have you seen the African daisy?
And the sunflower?
As they dance toward the sun
Each hour
a note

Then they close
when the conscious life force
folds his gentle arms
In warm peach and orange hues

Each sunset
his oeuvre
Ancient by design
we are swimming in the divine

Have you seen the ocean
That holds the earth in its depths
And judges not a soul that takes to
its shores in summer and spring

His clouds and sky
We see when we die
His ancient hand
Rests in the sand

His fingers dance
In our neurons
In memories
Of the ancient wisdom trees

Have you seen the tree that shelters
Its turtle dove and crow
equally in its leaves
not preferring black or white
Unkind is something impossible to conceive
When the cherry and almond trees
blossom

The cobalt blue night sky
of Van Gogh's Arles
Dripping with stars
Makes for wonder and delight
As our children
sleep tight.

for Lucy & Oscar

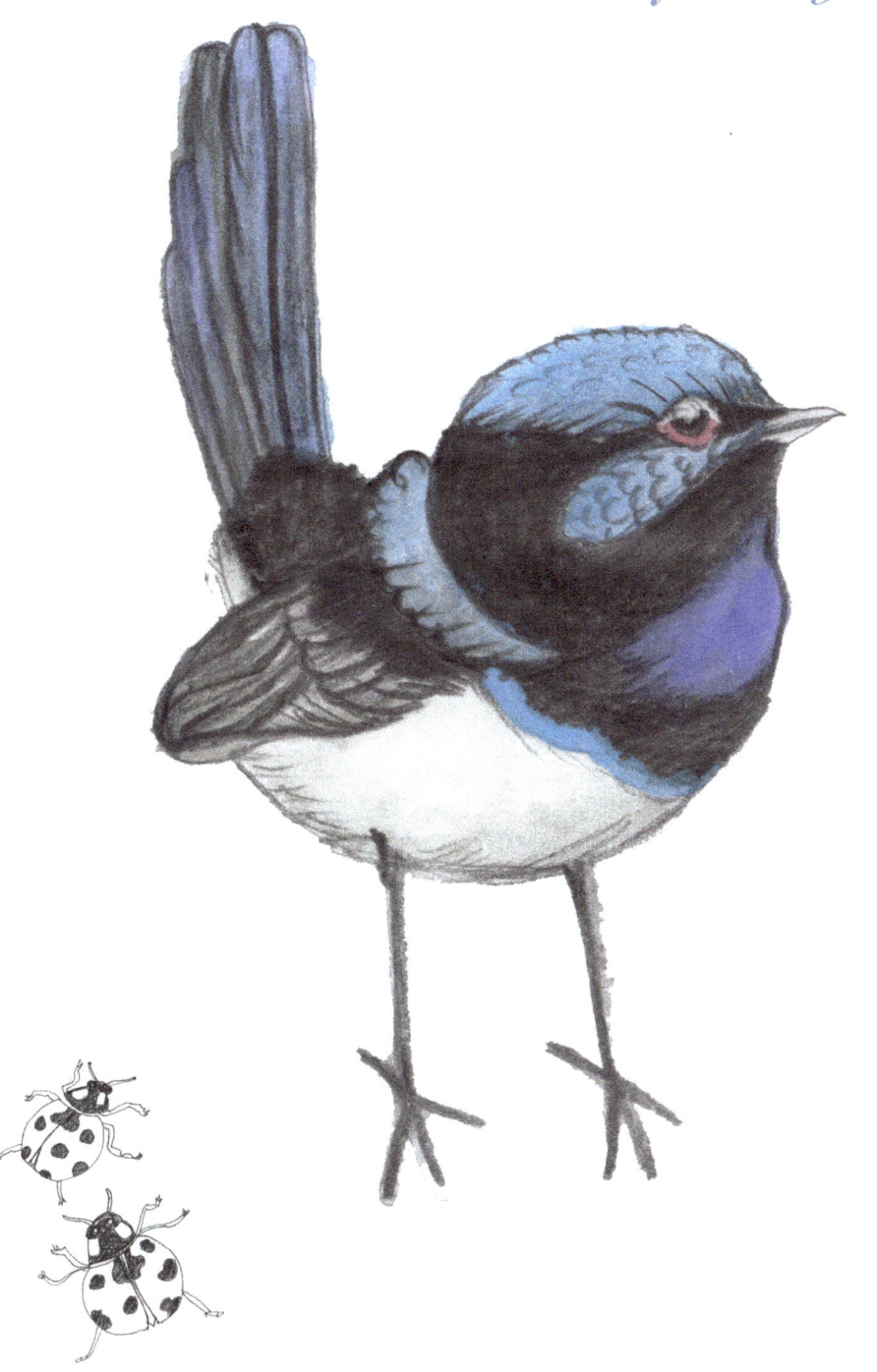

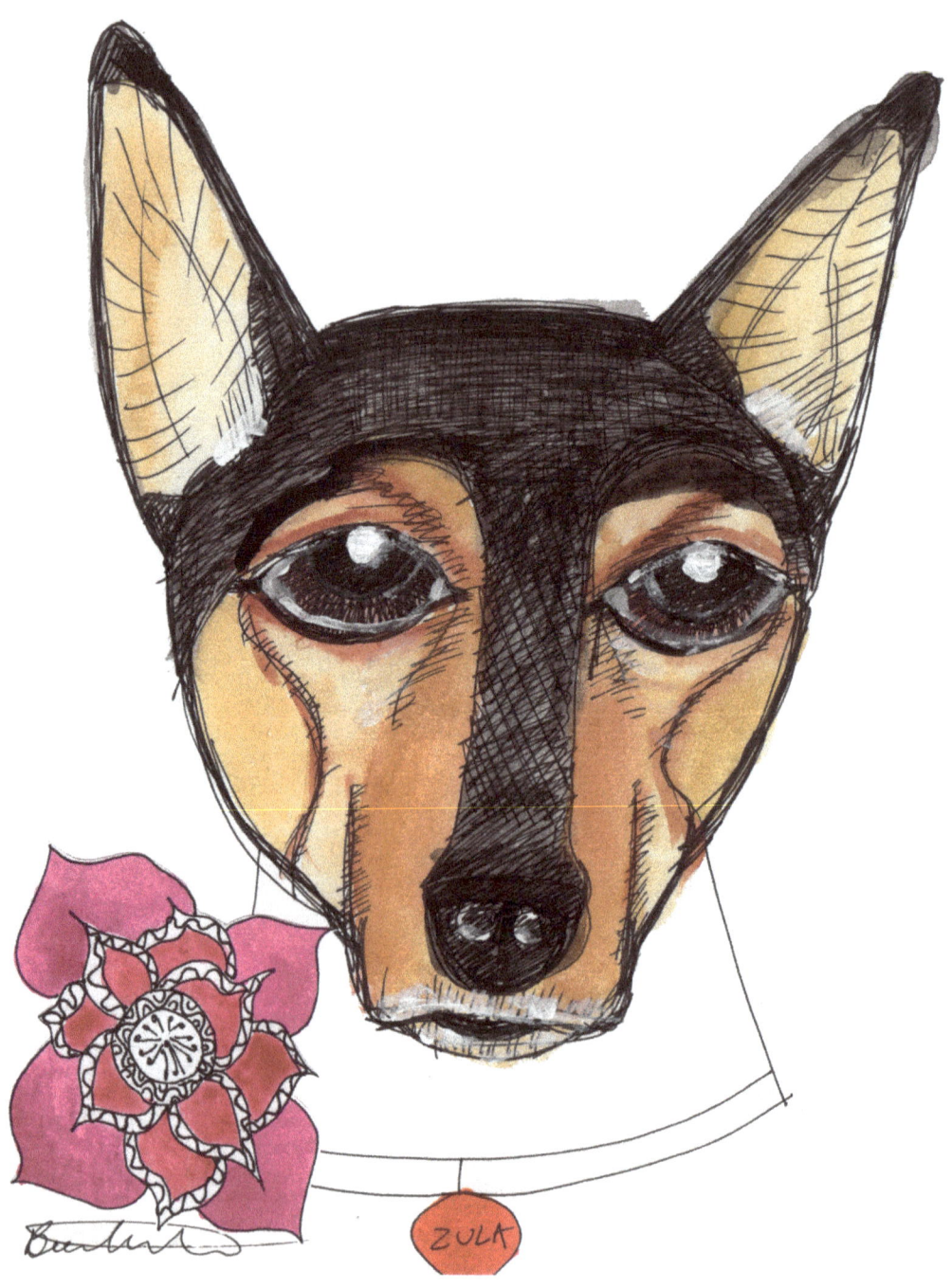

ZULA

Zula.

zula.

In my little faith
moments
That have stretched
To encompass years
I have found the soul
In her eyes
enough.

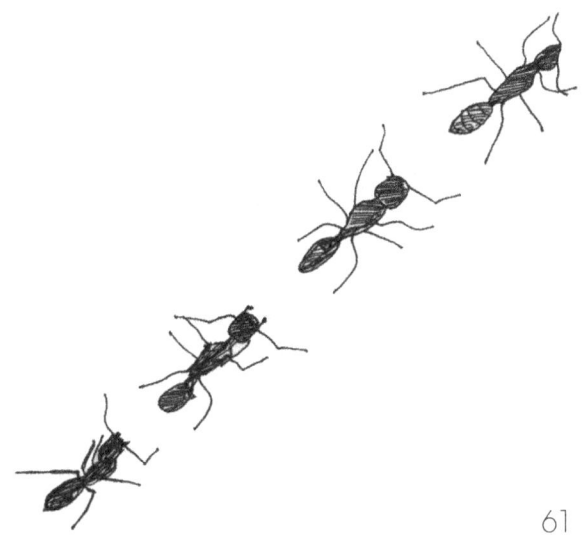

acknowledgements

To Carol for her undying love for my creative
pursuits and amazing talent for editing,
Kelly for her friendship & fine eyes for detail,
Charlotte for her encouragement and Jess
for the initial fire to my poetry flames at VCA.
Appreciation goes to Maribel for her support,
fantastic editing and wonderful friendship,
especially when I thought of giving up. A big
thank you goes to Sylvie at BookPOD for all
her help.

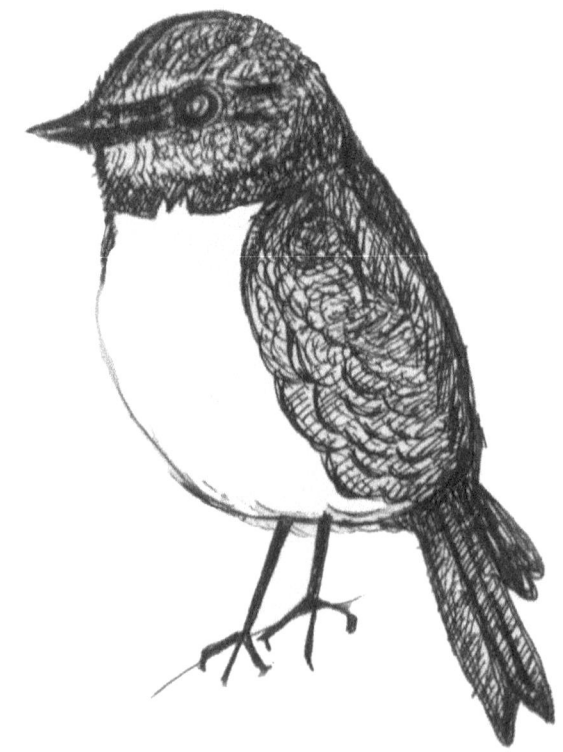

www.ingramcontent.com/pod-product-compliance
Lightning Source LLC
Chambersburg PA
CBHW041109280526
45792CB00011B/2360